CONTENTS

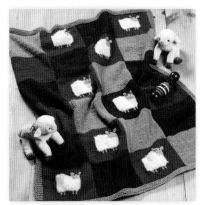

2   Go Baby **GO**

4   Golden **SLUMBERS**

5   Over the **RAINBOW**

6   Tickled **PINK**

8   Little Lamb **LULLABY**

9   Crisscross **BLANKET**

10   Hand-in-**HAND**

12   Hey Diddle **DIDDLE**

16   Cradle **COMFORT**

18   Her First **BLANKET**

21   His First **BLANKET**

22   Baby **LOVE**

24   Building **BLOCKS**

25   Pocket Full of **POSIES**

26   Heirloom **SAMPLER**

29   Octagonal **LACE**

30   Counting **SHEEP**

31   Sweet **SAFARI**

32   Mitered Square **THROW**

34   Lincoln **LOGS**

35   Mistral **THROW**

38   Felted **BLANKET**

39   Textured **BLANKET**

40   Diamond **THROW**

42   Cute **CRITTERS**

44   Patchwork **PERFECTION**

46   Barn **DANCE**

48   Lace Christening **BLANKET**

50   Sweet **DREAMS**

52   Lattice **DIAMONDS**

54   Whale's **TALE**

56   Hugs and **KISSES**

For pattern inquiries, please visit: www.go-crafty.com

Go Baby GO

YOU'LL NEED

YARN:  10½oz/300g, 330yd/300m of any super-bulky weight wool in red (A) and royal blue (C)

7oz/200g, 220yd/200m in chartreuse (B), gold (E), light blue (F), fuchsia (G), and black (H)

3½oz/100g, 110yd/100m in cream (J), grey (I) and purple (D)

NEEDLES: Size 10 (6mm) knitting needles *or size to obtain gauge*

ADDITIONAL: Size J/10 (6mm) crochet hook, tapestry needle

For windows: use (J)
For tires: use (H)
For bumpers, use (I)

KNITTED MEASUREMENTS

• 36" x 53"/194cm x 135cm (including crochet edging)

GAUGE

13 sts and 18 rows to 4"/10cm on size 10 (6mm) needles in St st.
Take time to check gauge.

Notes
1. Afghan is worked in one piece. Use a separate length of yarn for each block of color.
2. When changing yarns on same row, bring new color under old color to twist yarns to prevent holes.
3. Always work last row on each block in rev St st.

STITCH GLOSSARY

Seed Stitch
Row 1 (RS) *K1, p1; rep from * to end.
Row 2 *P1, k1; rep from * to end. Rep these 2 rows for seed st.
Garter ridge
*5 rows St st, 1 row rev St st; rep from * (6 rows) for garter ridge.

AFGHAN

With size 10 (6mm) needles and A, cast on 116 sts. K 2 rows.
Beg chart
Next row (RS) K20 sts with B, k19 with C, k19A, k19D, k19E, k20C. Cont in chart pat as established, k first and last st of every row for selvage st, through chart row 52, then rep rows 1–52 three times more, work rows 1–26 once. Change to A and k 2 rows. Bind off all sts with A.

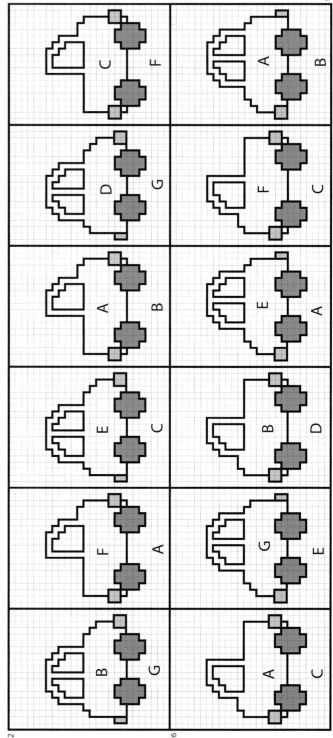

FINISHING

With tapestry needle, work 1 cross st in center of each wheel, choosing colors as desired. With A, work 1 cross st at intersection of all squares. With crochet hook and A, work 1 row of sc evenly around edge of afghan, then work 1 row of backwards sc. Fasten off.

Golden SLUMBERS

KNITTED MEASUREMENTS
• 32"x 42"/81.5cm x 106.5cm

GAUGE
12 sts and 18 rows to 4"/10cm over all pats using size 7 (4.5mm) needles. *Take time to check gauge.*

BLANKET
Cast on 84 sts.
Row 1 *K1, p1; rep from *.
Row 2 *P1, k1; rep from *.
Rep rows 1 and 2 three times more.
Next row [K1, p1] 3 times, k to last 6 sts, [k1, p1] 3 times.
Next row [P1, k1] 3 times, p to last 6 sts, [p1, k1] 3 times.

Pattern A
Row 3 (RS) [K1, p1] 3 times, [k8, p2, k8] 4 times, [k1, p1] 3 times.
Row 4 [P1, k1] 3 times, [p7, k4, p7] 4 times, [p1, k1] 3 times.
Row 5 [K1, p1] 3 times, [p1, k5, p2, k2, p2, k5, p1] 4 times, [k1, p1] 3 times.
Row 6 [P1, k1] 3 times, [k2, p3, k2, p4, k2, p3, k2] 4 times, [p1, k1] 3 times.
Row 7 [K1, p1] 3 times, [p1, k3, p2, k6, p2, k3, p1] 4 times, [k1, p1] 3 times.
Row 8 [P1, k1] 3 times, [p3 [k2, p3] 3 times] 4 times, [p1, k1] 3 times.
Row 9 [K1, p1] 3 times, [k2, p2, k3, p4, k3, p2, k2] 4 times, [k1, p1] 3 times.
Row 10 [P1, k1] 3 times, [p1, k2, [p5, k2] twice, p1] 4 times, [p1, k1] 3 times.
Row 11 [K1, p1] 3 times, [p2, k14, p2] 4 times, [k1, p1] 3 times.

Row 12 [P1, k1] 3 times, [k1, p16, k1] 4 times, [p1, k1] 3 times.
Rep rows 3–12 three times more.
Next row [K1, p1] 3 times, k to last 6 sts, [k1, p1] 3 times.
Next row [P1, k1] 3 times, p to last 6 sts, dec 2 sts evenly across row, [p1, k1] 3 times—82 sts.

Pattern B
Row 13 (RS) [K1, p1] 3 times, k4 [p2, k4] 11 times, [k1, p1] 3 times.
Row 14 [P1, k1] 3 times, p4, [k2, p4] 11 times, [p1, k1] 3 times.
Row 15 Rep row 13.
Row 16 Rep row 14.
Row 17 [K1, p1] 3 times, p1, k2, [p4, k2] 11 times, p1, [k1, p1] 3 times.

Row 18 [P1, k1] 3 times, k1, p2, [k4, p2] 11 times, k1, [p1, k1] 3 times.
Row 19 Rep row 17.
Row 20 Rep row 18.
Row 21 [K1, p1] 3 times, p to last 6 sts, [k1, p1] 3 times.
Row 22 [P1, k1] 3 times, k to last 6 sts, [p1, k1] 3 times.
Rep rows 13–22 once more.
Next row [K1, p1] 3 times, k to last 6 sts, [k1, p1] 3 times.
Next row [P1, k1] 3 times, p to last 6 sts, inc 2 sts evenly across row, [p1, k1] 3 times—84 sts.
Rep pats A and B once more, then rep pat A once.
Work rows 1 and 2 four times more. Bind off in rib.

Rose Callahan

Over the RAINBOW

YOU'LL NEED

YARN:  2¾oz/75g, 210yd/190m of any bulky weight wool blend in raspberry (A), gold (B), pastel yellow (C), pastel blue (E), teal (F), and chartreuse (G)

3oz/100g, 280yd/260m in natural (D)

NEEDLES/HOOKS: Size 6 (4mm) knitting needles *or size to obtain gauge*

Size G-6 (4mm) crochet hook

KNITTED MEASUREMENTS
• 24"x 36"/61cm x 91.5cm

GAUGE
19 sts and 41 rows to 4"/10cm over garter st using size 6 (4mm) needles. *Take time to check gauge.*

STRIPE PATTERN
Work 10 rows each in A, B, C, D, E, F, G. These 70 rows make up the stripe pat.

BLANKET
Increase slanted edge
With A, cast on 3 sts. Working in stripe pat and garter st, knit 1 row.
Next row K1, M1, k to end.
Rep last row until slanted edge measures 23"/58.5cm.

Diagonal
Next row K1, M1, k to end.
Next row K1, k2tog, k to end.
Rep last 2 rows until piece measures approx 35"/89cm from bottom short edge.

Decrease Slanted Edge
Next row K1, k2tog, k to end.
Rep last row until 3 sts rem. Bind off.

BORDER
With RS facing, crochet hook and D, work 3 rnds of sc evenly around outside edge of blanket. Fasten off.

Rose Callahan

Tickled PINK

YOU'LL NEED

YARN:  5¼oz/150g, 420yd/390m of any DK weight wool in dark lilac (A), dark pink (B), pink (C), and lilac (D

NEEDLES: One pair size 5 (3.75mm) needles *or size to obtain gauge*

ADDITIONAL: Size E/4 (3.5mm) crochet hook

KNITTED MEASUREMENTS
• 34 x 25"/86 x 63.5cm

GAUGE
22 sts and 24 rows to 4"/10cm over garter st using size 5 (3.75mm) needles.
Take time to check gauge

BLANKET

Petal square
(Knit 12 squares of each color)
Beg at corner with raised petal, cast on 4 sts.
Row 1 (RS) Ktbl across.
Row 2 K2, yo, k2.
Row 3 and every RS row through row 17 Knit. **Row 4** K2, yo, k1, yo, k2.
Row 6 K2, yo, k1, yo, p1, yo, k1, yo, k2.
Row 8 K2, yo, k1, p2, yo, p1, yo, p2, k1, yo, k2—15 sts.
Row 10 K2, yo, k2, p3, yo, p1, yo, p3, k2, yo, k2—19 sts. **Row 12** K2, yo, k3, p4, yo, p1, yo, p4, k3, yo, k2—23 sts. **Row 14** K2, yo, k4, p5, yo, p1, yo, p5, k4, yo, k2—27 sts. **Row 16** K2, yo, k5, p6, yo, p1, yo, p6, k5, yo, k2—31 sts. **Row 18** K2, yo, k6, p7, yo, p1, yo, p7, k6, yo, k2—35 sts. **Row 19** K9, SKP, k13, k2tog, k9—33 sts.
Row 20 K2, yo, k7, p15, k7, yo, k2—35 sts. **Row 21** K10, SKP, k11, k2tog, k10—33 sts. **Row 22** K2, yo, k8, p13, k8, yo, k2—35 sts. **Row 23** K11, SKP, k9, k2tog, k11—33 sts. **Row 24** K2, yo, k9, p11, k9, yo, k2—35 sts. **Row 25** K12, SKP, k7, k2tog, k12—33sts. **Row 26** K2, yo, k10, p9, k10, yo, k2—35 sts. **Row 27** K13, SKP, k5, k2tog, k13—33 sts. **Row 28** K2, yo, k11, p7, k11, yo, k2—35 sts.
Row 29 K14, SKP, k3, k2tog, k14—33 sts.
Row 30 K2, yo, k12, p5, k12, yo, k2—35 sts. **Row 31** K15, SKP, k1, k2tog, k15—33 sts. **Row 32** K2, yo, k13, p3, k13, yo, k2—35 sts. **Row 33** K16, SK2P, k16—33 sts.
Row 34 K2, yo, k29, yo, k2—35 sts. This completes ½ of square. Dec as foll:
Row 35 K3, k2tog, k25, k2tog, k3—33 sts. **Row 36** K2, yo, k2tog, k25, k2tog, yo, k2. **Row 37** K3, k2tog, k23, k2tog, k3—31 sts. **Row 38** K2, yo, k2tog, k23, k2tog, yo, k2. **Row 39** K3, k2tog, k21, k2tog, k3—29 sts. **Row 40** K2, yo, k2tog, k21, k2tog, yo, k2. **Row 41** K3, k2tog, k19, k2tog, k3—27 sts.

Row 42 K2, yo, k2tog, k19, k2tog, yo, k2.
Row 43 K3, k2tog, k17, k2tog, k3—25 sts. **Row 44** K2, yo, k2tog, k17, k2tog, yo, k2. **Row 45** K3, k2tog, k15, k2tog, k3—23 sts. **Row 46** K2, yo, k2tog, k15, k2tog, yo, k2. **Row 47** K3, k2tog, k13, k2tog, k3—21 sts. **Row 48** K2, yo, k2tog, k13, k2tog, yo, k2. **Row 49** K3, k2tog, k11, k2tog, k3—19 sts.
Row 50 K2, yo, k2tog, k11, k2tog, yo, k2.
Row 51 K3, k2tog, k9, k2tog, k3—17 sts.
Row 52 K2, yo, k2tog, k9, k2tog, yo, k2.
Row 53 K3, k2tog, k7, k2tog, k3—15 sts.
Row 54 K2, yo, k2tog, k7, k2tog, yo, k2.
Row 55 K3, k2tog, k5, k2tog, k3—13 sts.
Row 56 K2, yo, k2tog, k5, k2tog, yo, k2.
Row 57 K3, k2tog, k3, k2tog, k3—11 sts.
Row 58 K2, yo, k2tog, k3, k2tog, yo, k2.
Row 59 K3, k2tog, k1, k2tog, k3—9 sts.
Row 60 K2, yo, k2tog, k1, k2tog, yo, k2.
Row 61 K3, k2tog, k1, k3.
Row 62 K2, yo, k2tog twice, yo, k2.
Row 63 K3, k2tog, k3.
Row 64 K2tog 3 times, k1.
Bind off.

FINISHING
Foll diagram, sew squares tog.

Crochet edging
Rnd 1 With RS of blanket facing, attach D to side edging. Ch 1, sc in same space, sc in every st to corner, 3 sc in corner, sc to first sc. With C, sl st into first sc.
Rnd 2 Sc in back loop of first sc, *long sc in sc of first row (by working into base of sc, not top lp), sc in back loop of next sc, rep from * to corner, at corner, work long sc, ch2, long sc; cont in this way around.

Petal Square
make 12

Color A = Dark lilac
Color B = Dark pink
Color C = Pink
Color D = Lilac

Jose Santa

Little Lamb LULLABY

YOU'LL NEED

YARN:  7oz/200g, 420yd/380m of any DK weight wool in royal blue (A) and green (B)

5¼oz/150g, 315yd/290m in red (C)

1¾oz/50g, 110yd/100m in tan (D)

1¾oz/50g, 100yd/95m of any DK weight wool bouclé in white (E)

NEEDLES: One pair size 6 (4mm) needles *or size to obtain gauge.*

ADDITIONAL: Size F/5 (4mm) crochet hook, bobbins (optional)

KNITTED MEASUREMENTS

• 27"x 36"/68.5cm x 91cm

GAUGE

20 sts and 26 rows to 4"/10cm over St st using size 6 (4mm) needles.
Take time to check gauge.

Notes

1. Blanket is worked in one piece or it may be worked in 4 separate strips and sewn tog.
2. Use a separate ball of yarn for each block of color Use a separate ball/bobbin of B for garter st edges.
3. When changing colors, twist yarns tog on WS to prevent holes.

AFGHAN

Cast on 5 sts B, 32 sts B, 32 sts A, 32 sts C, 32 sts A, 5 sts B—138 sts. Keeping the first and last 5 sts in garter st in B, work blocks in St st foll diagram for color and chart pat (each block is 32 sts and 36 rows). Bind off.

FINISHING

Block afghan. With RS facing and B, pick up 138 sts evenly along top and bottom edge. Work in garter st for 8 rows. Bind off.

Lamb

With A, work a French knot for eyes. With crochet hook and D, ch 8. Join with sl st to first ch. Sew center tog to close ear. See chart for placement.

Color Key

☐ Background color (MC)

⌇ French knot with Royal (A)

· Red (C)

☒ White (E)

⌀ Chain st with Caramel (D)

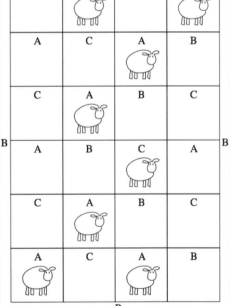

PLACEMENT DIAGRAM

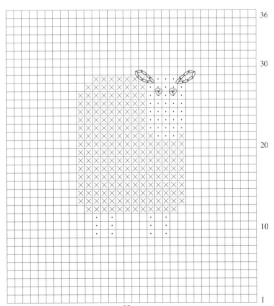

Crisscross BLANKET

YOU'LL NEED

YARN: 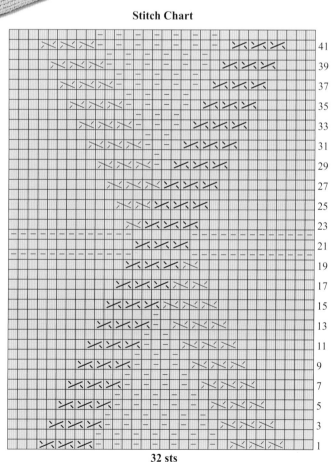 **5** 28oz/800g, 1080yd/980m of any bulky weight cotton/acrylic yarn in yellow

NEEDLES: One pair size 10 (6mm) needles *or size to obtain gauge*

KNITTED MEASUREMENTS

• 43" x 34"/109cm x 86cm

GAUGE

14 sts and 20 rows to 4"/10cm over St st using size 10 (6mm) needles.
Take time to check gauge.

Note

Blanket is made in separate squares, then sewn tog. Garter st edge is worked after squares are sewn tog.

STITCH GLOSSARY

Right Twist (RT)
K2tog but do not drop sts from needle, k first st once more, drop both sts from LH needle.

Left Twist (LT)
Skip first st on LH needle and k into back of 2nd st, then k2tog tbl and drop both sts from LH needle.

BLANKET

Squares (make 12)
Cast on 32 sts. P 1 row on WS. Work 42 rows in chart pat. K 1 row on RS. Bind off purlwise on WS.

FINISHING

Sew squares tog, 3 wide by 4 long, alternating the direction of each square (see photo).

Borders

Block to measurements. With RS facing, pick up and k 126 sts along each long edge. Work in garter st for 4"/10cm, end with a RS row. Bind off knitwise on WS. With RS facing, pick up and k 120 sts evenly along other two edges, including sides of border. Work in garter st for 4"/10cm, end with a RS row. Bind off knitwise on WS.

Quenet

Stitch Chart

Stitch key

☐ K on RS, p on WS

− P on RS, k on WS

⬛ RT

⬛ LT

32 sts

41 39 37 35 33 31 29 27 25 23 21 19 17 15 13 11 9 7 5 3 1

YOU'LL NEED

YARN: (3) 7oz/200g, 560yd/500m of any DK weight wool yarn in gold (MC)

5¼oz/150g, 420yd/370m of any DK weight wool yarn in both orange (A) and dk blue (B)

3½oz/100g, 280yd/250m of any DK weight wool yarn in both lt teal (C) and hot pink (D)

1¾oz/50g, 140yd/130m of any DK weight wool yarn in both magenta (E) and red (F)

NEEDLES: One pair each sizes 7 and 8 (4.5 and 5mm) needles *or size to obtain gauge*

KNITTED MEASUREMENTS
• 32" x 46"/81cm x 117cm

GAUGE
22 sts and 22 rows to 4"/10 cm over chart pats using size 8 (5mm) needles.
Take time to check gauge.

Note
When changing colors, twist yarns on WS row to prevent holes in work. Carry colors not in use loosely across back of work.

BLANKET
With larger needles and MC, cast on 163 sts. Work in St st and charts as foll:

Beg chart 1
Row 1 (RS) Work 6-st rep of chart 27 times, work last st once. Cont as established through row 8.

Beg chart 2
Row 1 (RS) Work first st of chart, work 16-st rep of chart 10 times, work last 2 sts once. Cont as established through row 16.

Beg chart 3
Row 1 (RS) Work 6-st rep of chart 27 times, work last st once. Cont as established through row 6.

Beg chart 4
Row 1 (RS) Work 6-st rep of chart 27 times, work last st once. Cont as established through row 4.

Beg chart 5
Row 1 (RS) Work first 7 sts, work 12-st rep of chart 13 times. Cont as established through row 12.

Beg charts 6-10
Beg and end same as charts 1-5, working colors as shown in corresponding charts.
Rep these 92 rows for pat until piece measures approx 43"/109cm from beg, end with row 7 of chart 6. P 1 row with MC. Bind off.

FINISHING
Block to measurements.

Garter St Border
With RS facing, smaller needles and MC, pick up and k 151 sts along cast-on edge. Work in garter st for 1½"/4cm, inc 1 st each side every RS row and sl the first st of every row wyib. Bind off knitwise on WS. Work in same way along bound-off edge.
With RS facing, smaller needles and MC, pick up and k 198 sts along each side edge and work garter st and inc's as before. Sew corners tog.

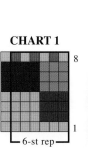

CHART 1

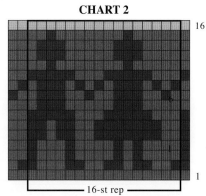

CHART 2

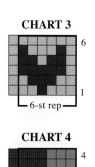

CHART 3

CHART 4

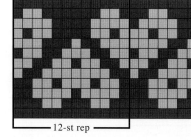

CHART 5

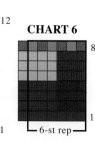

CHART 6

Quenet

Color key
- ☐ Gold (MC)
- ▦ Orange (A)
- ■ Dk blue (B)
- ▨ Lt teal (C)
- ▩ Hot pink (D)
- ■ Magenta (E)
- ■ Red (F)

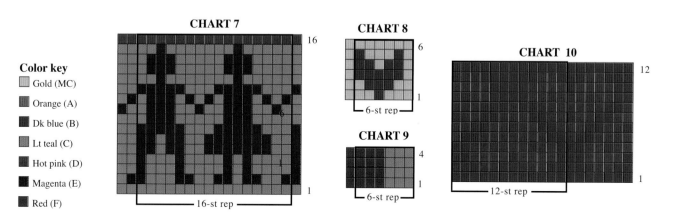

CHART 7

16

1

└─── 16-st rep ───┘

CHART 8

6

1

└─ 6-st rep ─┘

CHART 9

4

1

└─ 6-st rep ─┘

CHART 10

12

1

└─── 12-st rep ───┘

Hey DIDDLE DIDDLE

YOU'LL NEED

YARN: 3 21oz/600g, 1400yd/1280m of any DK weight cotton yarn each in white (MC)

1¾oz/50g, 116yd/106m of any DK weight cotton yarn each in pink (A), black (B), gold (C), med blue (D), turquoise (E), lilac (F) and pale yellow (G)

NEEDLES: Size 7 (4.5mm) circular needle, 32"/80cm long *or size to obtain gauge*

ADDITIONAL: Stitch markers and bobbins

KNITTED MEASUREMENTS

• 28¼" x 36¼"/72cm x 92cm

GAUGE

18 sts and 24 rows to 4"/10 cm over St st using size 7 (4.5mm) needles and 2 strands of yarn.
Take time to check gauge.

Note
Use 2 strands of yarn held tog throughout.

BLANKET

With 2 strands MC, cast on 127 sts.
Row 1 (RS) Work 72 sts of chart 1, then cont to work 18-st diamonds to end of row. Cont in pats as established, foll placement diagram for St st (blank) and seed st (shaded) diamonds and color charts. After all motifs have been worked (217 rows), bind off.

FINISHING

Block piece to measurements.
Using single strand, embroider stars with F, motif details with B and the fiddle's bow with a double strand of B.

Stitch key
☐ K on RS, p on WS
⊟ P on RS, k on WS

Color key
☐ White (MC)
▨ Pink (A)
▨ Black (B)
▨ Gold (C)
▨ Med blue (D)
▨ Turquoise (E)
▨ Lilac (F)
☐ Pale yellow (G)
✳ Star

CHART 1

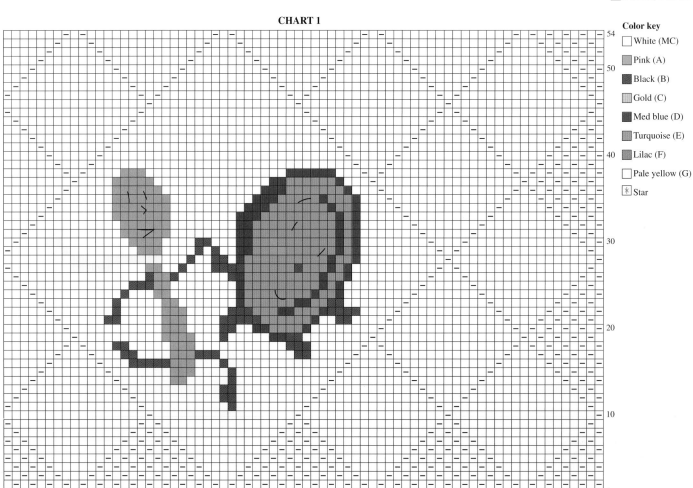

Quenet

CHART 2

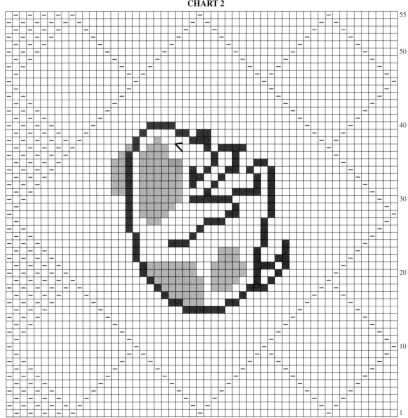

Stitch key

☐ K on RS, p on WS

⊟ P on RS, k on WS

Color key

☐ White (MC)

▨ Pink (A)

■ Black (B)

▨ Gold (C)

▨ Med blue (D)

▨ Turquoise (E)

▨ Lilac (F)

☐ Pale yellow (G)

⁎ Star

CHART 3

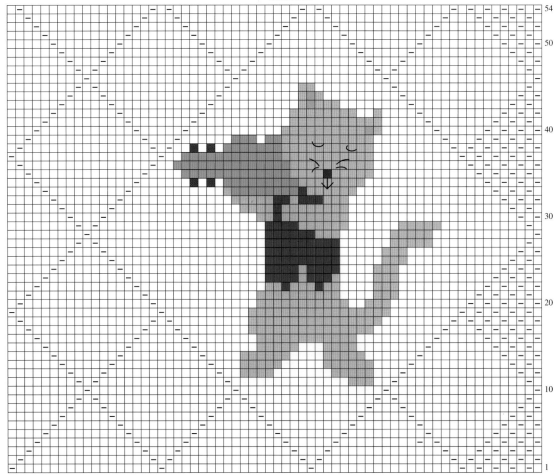

CHART 4

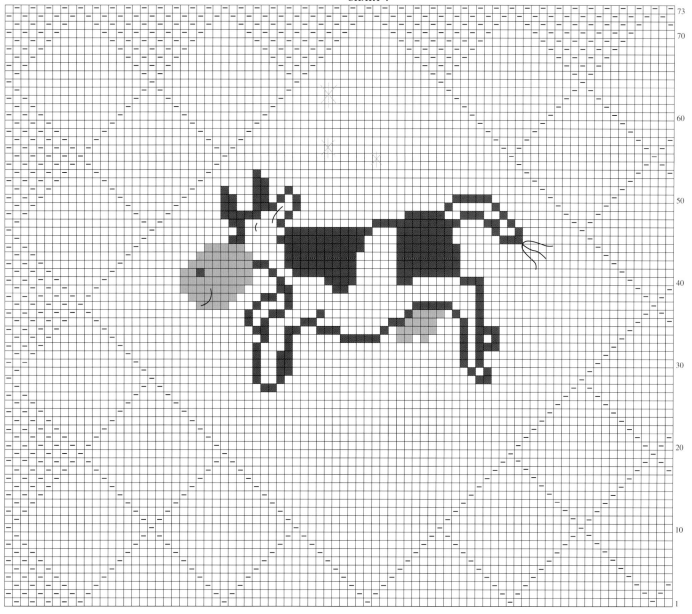

Color key

☐ White (MC)

▨ Pink (A)

■ Black (B)

▨ Gold (C)

▨ Med blue (D)

▨ Turquoise (E)

▨ Lilac (F)

☐ Pale yellow (G)

✳ Star

Stitch key

☐ K on RS, p on WS

— P on RS, k on WS

PLACEMENT DIAGRAM

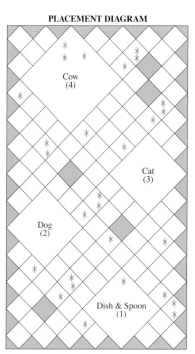

Cow
(4)

Cat
(3)

Dog
(2)

Dish & Spoon
(1)

Cradle COMFORT

YOU'LL NEED

YARN:  12¼oz/350g, 1250yd/ 1140m of any DK weight acrylic

NEEDLES: One pair size 5 (3.75mm) needles *or size to obtain gauge*

ADDITIONAL: Cable needle (cn)

KNITTED MEASUREMENTS

• 26" x 34"/66cm x 86cm

GAUGE

23 sts and 37 rows to 4"/10cm over chart pat using size 5 (3.75mm) needles. *Take time to check gauge.*

RIGHT CABLE PANEL

(over 9 sts, inc'd to 13)
Preparation row 1 (RS) K in front and back of next st, p in front and back of next st, k5, p in front and back of next st, k in front and back of next st.
Row 2 and all WS rows K the knit sts and p the purl sts.
Rows 3, 5, 9 and 11 K2, p2, k5, p2, k2.
Row 7 K2, p2, sl 2 sts to cn and hold to *back*, k3, k2 from cn, p2, k2.
Rep rows 2-11 for right cable panel.

LEFT CABLE PANEL

Work as for right cable panel, but work row 7 as foll: K2, p2, sl 3 sts to cn and hold to *front*, k2, k3 from cn, p2, k2.

Chart pat
Work all RS (odd-numbered) rows as foll: Beg with first st of chart, work to last st, skip last (center) st and work chart back from left to right to first st. P all WS rows.

AFGHAN

Cast on 147 sts and p 11 rows.

Beg pats
Next row (RS) P6, work 9 sts right cable panel, 117 sts chart pat, 9 sts left cable pat, p6—155 sts. Cont in pats as established, keeping first and last 6 sts as p every row, until 42 rows of chart pat have been worked 7 times. P next row, dec 4 sts over each cable panel—147 sts. P 9 rows more. Bind off all sts.

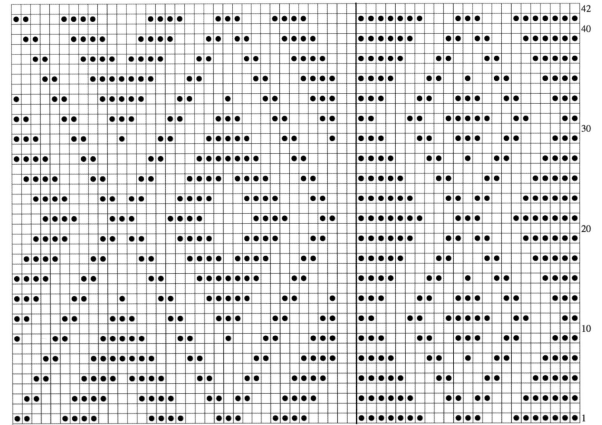

Stitch Key

☐ K on RS, p on WS

● P on RS, k on WS

↑Center st

Her First BLANKET

YOU'LL NEED

YARN:  3½oz/100g, 360yd/330m of any DK weight acrylic in dark pink (K)

1¾oz/50g, 180yd/160m in bright yellow (A), pale yellow (B), white (C), lt blue (E), med green (F), lime (G), purple (H), lavender (I), red (J), med pink (L), orange (N), med brown (O), and navy (P)

NEEDLES: One pair each sizes 5 and 6 (3.75 and 4mm) needles *or sizes to obtain gauge*

ADDITIONAL: 28" x 28"/71cm x 71cm square of flannel fabric for backing, tapestry needle

KNITTED MEASUREMENTS

• 28" x 28"/71cm x 71cm square

GAUGES

One plaid square, 31 sts and 40 rows to 5⅛"/13cm square using smaller needles. One St st square, 31 sts and 40 rows to 5⅛"/13cm square using larger needles. *Take time to check gauges*

AFGHAN

Note

When working plaid squares, carry color not in use to border sts each side to keep squares even.

Plaid squares (make 8)

With smaller needles and dk color, cast on 31 sts. Foll chart, k1 row p1 row. Then foll chart, work rows 3-14 once, [rows 7-14] 3 times. Work rows 15 and 16 with dk color. Bind off. Make 2 squares in each of the foll 4 color combinations:
1. Dk color = br yellow (A); lt color = yellow (B); white (C).
2. Dk color = red (J); lt color = orange (N); white (C).
3. Dk color = dk pink (K), lt color = med pink (L); white (C).
4. Dk color = purple (H); lt color = lavender (I); white (C).

Stockinette st square (make 17)

With larger needles, and given color, cast on 31 sts. Work in St st for 40 rows. Bind off. Make 3 squares in br yellow (A) (1 embroidered with cow); 1 square in yellow (B) (embroidered with horse); 2 squares in lt blue (E) (1 embroidered with roosters, 1 with pig); 2 squares in lime (G) (1 embroidered with cow, 1 with sheep); 3 squares in lavender (I) (1 embroidered with man); 1 square in med pink (L) (embroidered with woman); 3 squares in orange (N) (1 embroidered with cat, 1 with horse).

FINISHING

Block pieces lightly. Work duplicate st embroidery on squares foll charts, instructions and photo. Foll alternate chart colors for horse and sheep as in photo. Embroider eyes, tail, and other featured in straight st, stem st, and French knot as in photo. Embroider for square placement (including directions of squares), sew 5 rows of 5 squares each tog.

Edging

With smaller needles and K, cast on 14 sts.***Row 1 (RS)** P6, p2tog, yo, k3, yo, k2tog, k1. **Rows 2 and 4** P to last st, p into back and front of last st. **Row 3** P6, p2tog, yo, k4, yo, k2tog, k1. **Row 5** P6, p2tog, yo, k5, yo, k2tog, k1. **Row 6** Rep row 2—17sts. **Rows 7, 9, 11, 13, and 15** P6, p2tog, yo ,k6, yo, k2tog, k1.
Rows 8, 10, 12, 14, 16, 18, 20, and 22 P all sts. **Row 17** P2tog, p5, p2tog, yo, k5, yo k2tog, k1. **Row 19** P2tog, p5, p2tog, yo, k4, yo, k2tog, k1. **Row 21** P2tog, p5, p2tog, yo, k3, yo, k2tog, k1—14 sts. Rep rows 1-22 9 times more. (Edging fits along one side of afghan.)

Shape Corner

Row 1 P6, p2tog, yo, k3, yo, k2tog, sl 1 wyif. **Row 2** Sl 1, sl 1 wyif, p11, p into back and front of next st. **Row 3** P6, p2tog, yo, k4, sl 1 wyif, turn. **Row 4** Sl 1, p11, p into back and front of next st. **Row 5** P6, p2tog, yo, k4, sl 1 wyif, turn. **Row 6** Sl 1, p11, p into back and front of next st. **Row 7** P6, p2tog, yo, k4, sl 1, wyif, turn. **Rows 8, 10, 12, 13, 16, 18, 20, 22, and 24** Sl 1, p to end. **Row 9** P6, p2tog, yo, k3, sl 1 wyif, turn. **Row 11** P6, p2tog, yo, k2, sl 1, wyif, turn. **Row 13** P6, p2tog, yo, k1, sl 1, wyif, turn. **Row 15** P6,

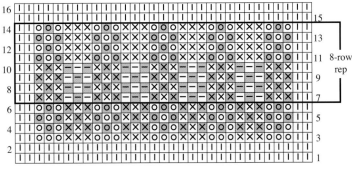

PLAID SQUARE

8-row rep

Stitch & Color key
- I Dk. color, k on RS, p on WS
- − Dk. color, k on RS, p on WS
- = Dk. color, p on RS, k on WS
- ⊠ Lt. color, k on RS, p on WS
- ⊠ Lt. color, p on RS, k on WS
- O White, k on RS, p on WS
- O White, p on RS, k on WS

p2tog, yo, sl 1 wyif, turn. **Row 17** P7, sl 1 wyif, turn. **Row 19** P2tog, p4, sl 1 wyif, turn. **Row 21** P2tog, p2, sl 1 wyif, turn. **Row 23** P2tog, sl 1 wyif, turn. **Row 25** P3, sl1 wyif, turn. **Row 27** P5, sl 1 wyif, turn. **Rows 26, 28, and 30** P to last st, p into back and front of last st. **Row 27** P5, sl 1 wyif, turn. **Row 29** P7, sl1 wyif, turn. **Row 31** P6, p2tog, yo, k1, sl 1 wyif, turn. **Rows 32, 34, 36, 38, 40, 42, 44, 46, and 48** Purl. **Row 33** P6, p2tog, yo, k2, sl1 wyif, turn. **Row 35** P6, p2tog, yo, k3, sl 1 wyif, turn. **Row 37** P6, p2tog, yo, k4, sl 1 wyif, turn. **Row 39** P6, p2tog, yo, k5, sl 1 wyif, turn. **Row 41** P6, p1tog, yo, k6, sl 1 wyif, turn. **Row 43** P2tog, p5, p2tog, yo, k6, sl 1 wyif, turn. **Row 45** P2tog, p5, p2tog, yo, k4, yo, k2tog, k1. **Row 47** P2tog, p5, p2tog, yo, k3, yo, k2tog, k1.* Rep between *'s 3 times more. Bind off. Sew edging in place around outside of afghan. Embroider lazy daisy flowers as in photo. Fold in backing fabric for ½"/1.5cm and sew to WS of afghan with thread, inside edging.

Brian Kraus

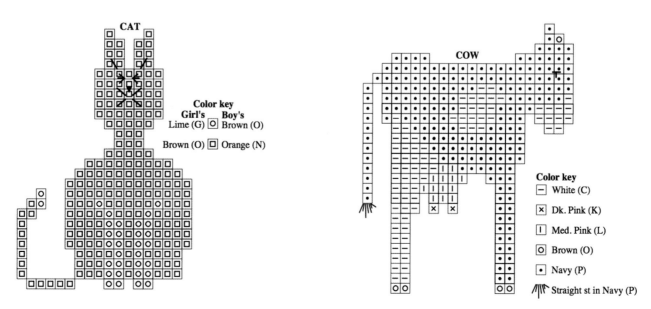

CAT

Color key

Girl's   **Boy's**

Lime (G) ⊙ Brown (O)

Brown (O) ☐ Orange (N)

COW

Color key

─ White (C)

☒ Dk. Pink (K)

❘ Med. Pink (L)

⊙ Brown (O)

• Navy (P)

⫽⫽⫽ Straight st in Navy (P)

MAN

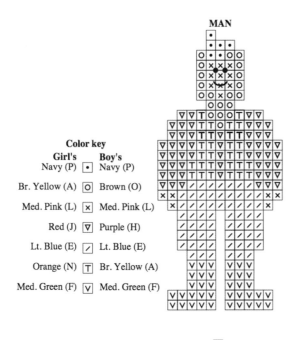

Color key

	Girl's		Boy's
	Navy (P)	•	Navy (P)
	Br. Yellow (A)	O	Brown (O)
	Med. Pink (L)	×	Med. Pink (L)
	Red (J)	▽	Purple (H)
	Lt. Blue (E)	∕	Lt. Blue (E)
	Orange (N)	T	Br. Yellow (A)
	Med. Green (F)	⋁	Med. Green (F)

ROOSTER

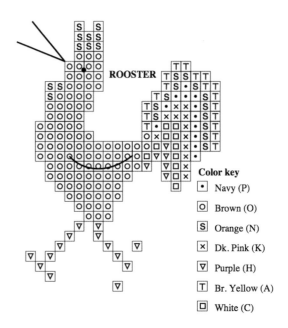

Color key

•	Navy (P)
O	Brown (O)
S	Orange (N)
×	Dk. Pink (K)
▽	Purple (H)
T	Br. Yellow (A)
□	White (C)

HORSE

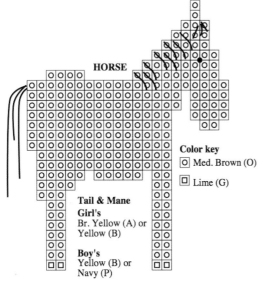

Color key

O	Med. Brown (O)
□	Lime (G)

Tail & Mane
Girl's
Br. Yellow (A) or
Yellow (B)

Boy's
Yellow (B) or
Navy (P)

SHEEP

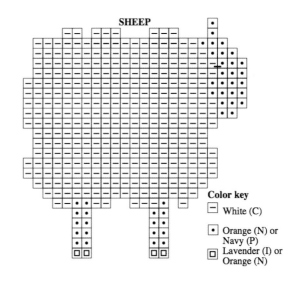

Color key

−	White (C)
•	Orange (N) or Navy (P)
□	Lavender (I) or Orange (N)

WOMAN

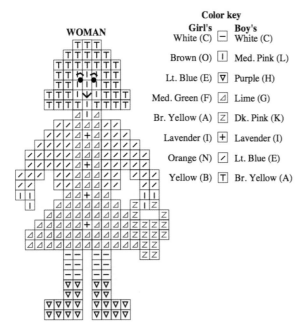

Color key

	Girl's		Boy's
	White (C)	−	White (C)
	Brown (O)	I	Med. Pink (L)
	Lt. Blue (E)	▽	Purple (H)
	Med. Green (F)	⟋	Lime (G)
	Br. Yellow (A)	Z	Dk. Pink (K)
	Lavender (I)	+	Lavender (I)
	Orange (N)	∕	Lt. Blue (E)
	Yellow (B)	T	Br. Yellow (A)

PIG

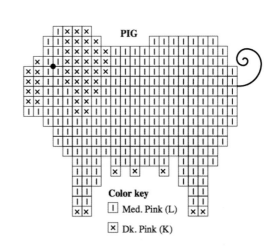

Color key

I	Med. Pink (L)
×	Dk. Pink (K)

His First BLANKET

YOU'LL NEED

YARN: 🧶 **3** 3½oz/100g, 360yd/330m of any DK weight acrylic in navy (P)

1¾oz/50g, 180yd/160m in bright yellow (A), pale yellow (B), white (C), med blue (D), lt blue (E), med green (F), lime (G), purple (H), lavender (I), dk pink (K), med pink (L), orange (N) and med brown (O)

NEEDLES: One pair each sizes 5(3.75mm) and 6(4mm) needles *or sizes to obtain gauge*

ADDITIONAL: Size C/2 (2.5mm) crochet hook, 30" x 30"/75cm x 75cm square of flannel fabric for backing , tapestry needle

KNITTED MEASUREMENTS

• 27" x 27"/68.5cm x 68.5cm

GAUGES

One plaid square, 31 sts and 40 rows to 5"/13cm square using size 5 (3.75mm) needles.
One St st square, 31 sts and 40 rows to 5"/13cm square using size 6 (4mm) needles.
Take time to check gauges

Note

When working plaid squares, carry color not in use to border sts each side to keep squares even.

AFGHAN

Plaid squares (make 8)
With size 5 (3.75mm) needles and dk color, cast on 31 sts. Foll chart, k1 row, p1 row. Then foll chart, work rows 3-14 once, [rows 7-14] 3 times. Work rows 15 and 16 with dk color. Bind off.
Make 2 squares in each of the foll 4 color combinations:
1. Dk color = br yellow (A); lt color = yellow (B); white (C).
2. Dk color = med blue (D), lt color =

lt blue (E); white (C).
3. Dk color = med green (F); lt color = lime (G); white (C).
4. Dk color = purple (H); lt color = lavender (I); white (C).

Stockinette st square (make 17)
With size 6 (4mm) needles and given color, cast on 31 sts. Work in St st for 40 rows. Bind off. Make 2 squares in br yellow (A) (1 embroidered with pig); 2 squares in yellow (B) (1 embroidered with horse, 1 with cat); 2 squares in med blue (D); 1 square in med green (F) (embroidered with sheep); 2 squares in lime (G) (1 embroidered with rooster, 1 with cow); 3 squares in purple (H) (1 embroidered with horse); 1 square in lavender (I) (embroidered with cow); 2 squares in navy (P) (1 embroidered with sheep, 1 with pig); 2 squares in orange (N) (1 embroidered with man, 1 with woman).

FINISHING

Block pieces lightly. Work duplicate stitch embroidery on squares foll charts. Foll alternate chart colors for horse and sheep as in photo. Embroider eyes, tails and other features in straight st, stem st and

French knot as in photo. Embroider sheep with random French knots. Foll photo for square placement (including direction of squares), sew 5 rows of 5 squares each tog.

Border

Border is worked using colors in a random order having stripes that are 2 or 4 rows wide, as desired, in pat as foll: With size 5 (3.75mm) needles, cast on 9 sts. K2 rows, * work 5 rows in St st, k next WS row; rep from * until border fits along one side of afghan plus 1"/2.5cm to fit cast-on edge of next border. Work 3 more borders in same way. Sew borders in place around outside.

Crochet edge

With crochet hook and P, sc evenly around border of afghan, working 2 sc in each corner. Join and ch 1, and work 4 more rnds of sc in each sc. Fasten off. Fold in backing fabric for ½"/1.5cm and sew to WS of afghan.

Baby LOVE

YOU'LL NEED

YARN: [5] *Jiffy* by Lion Brand Co., 3oz/85g, 135yd/124m acrylic
2 skeins each sienna (A), country green (B) and melon (G)

1 skein each lilac (F), denim heather (E), silver (J), dusty rose (D), golden rod (C), rose (H) and taupe (I)

NEEDLES: Size 10 (6mm) knitting needles *or size to obtain gauge*

ADDITIONAL: Size J/10 (6mm) crochet hook, tapestry needle

KNITTED MEASUREMENTS

• 37" x 45"/94cm x 114cm (including crochet edging)

GAUGE

13 sts and 19 rows to 4"/10cm on size 10 needles in St st.
Take time to check gauge

STITCH GLOSSARY

Seed St
Row 1 (RS) *K1, p1; rep from * to end.
Row 2 *P1, k1; rep from * to end.
Rep last 2 rows for seed st.
Ridge Pat #1
*3 rows St st, 1 row rev St st; rep from *.
Ridge Pat #2
*2 rows St st, 2 rows rev St st.

Note
Afghan is worked in one piece. Use a separate length of yarn for each block of color. When changing yarns on same row, bring new color under old color and twist yarns to prevent holes.

SQUARES
1. Background: St st with B; Heart: St st with D; Embroidery: Horizontal ch st with F, vertical ch st with E, straight st with G.
2. Background: Seed st with C; Heart: St st with E; Embroidery: French knots with G.
3. Background: St st with D; Heart: rev St st with H; Embroidery: Cross st with J.
4. Background: Ridge pat #1 with E; Heart: Ridge Pat #2 with A; Embroidery: Running st (over 2 rows, under 2 rows) with B.
5. Background: Ridge Pat #1 with A; Heart: rev St st with I; Embroidery: Running st with C

6. Background: St st with F; Heart: Seed st with G; Embroidery: Straight st with D.
7. Background: Garter st with B; Heart: St st with J; Embroidery: French knots with A.
8. Background: St st with G; Heart: St st with C; Embroidery: Diamonds in straight st with F, around heart straight st with E and French knots with D.
9. Background: Garter st #1 with G; Heart: St st with J; Embroidery: Straight st with E.
10. Background: Ridge pat #1 with H; Heart: Seed st with B; Embroidery: Chain st with F.
11. Background: St st with C; Heart: St st with D; Embroidery: Chain st with G, Running st with B.
12. Background: Seed st with I; Heart: St st with F; Embroidery: Straight st with J.

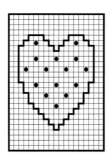 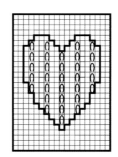 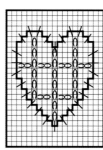 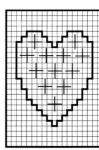

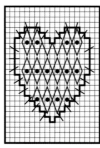 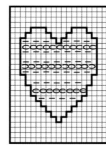 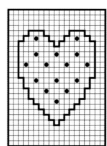 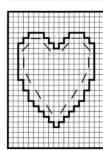

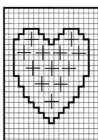 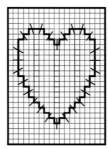  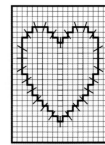

Straight st
Running st
Chain st
French knot

Andy Cohen

AFGHAN

With size 10 (6mm) needles and A, cast on 135 sts. K 2 rows.

Beg Pats—Next row (RS) K20 sts with B, k19 with C, k19D, k19E, k19D, k19C, k20B. Cont in chart pat as established, k first and last st of every row for selvage st, working individual Heart charts as described and foll placement chart. Change to A and k 2 rows. Bind off all sts with A.

FINISHING

With tapestry needle and A, work 1 cross st at intersection of all squares. With crochet hook and A, work 1 row of sc evenly around edge of afghan, then work 1 row of backwards sc (from left to right). Fasten off.

**Heart Afghan
Placement Chart**

#9	#10	#11	#12	#11	#10	#9
#5	#6	#7	#8	#7	#6	#5
#1	#2	#3	#4	#3	#2	#1

rep 3 times

work 1 time

Building BLOCKS

Quenet

YOU'LL NEED

YARN:  10½oz/300g, 750yd/ of any worsted weight wool blend yarn

NEEDLES: One size 6 (4mm) circular needle 29"/74cm long *or size to obtain gauge*

KNITTED MEASUREMENTS
• 32" x 32"/81.5cm x 81.5cm

GAUGE
22 sts and 30 rows to 4"/10cm over St st using size 6 (4mm) needles.
Take time to check gauge.

Note
For selvages, slip first st of every row purlwise with yarn in front, then take yarn to back between needles, k last st of every row.

STITCH GLOSSARY
Eyelet Panel (worked across 9 sts)
Rows 1-4 Knit.
Row 5 (WS) K2, [k2tog, yo] twice, k3.
Rows 6-8 Knit.
Row 9 K1, [k2tog, yo] 3 times, k2.
Rows 10-12 Knit.
Rows 13-16 Rep rows 5-8.
Rep rows 1 - 16 for eyelet panel.

BLANKET
Cast on 11 sts. Keeping first and last sts as selvage, work 16

rows of eyelet panel over center 9 sts.
Next row (WS) Cast on 9 sts and work as foll: 1 selvage st, row 1 of eyelet panel over next 9 sts, k9 (for rev St st block), 1 selvage st—20 sts.
Next row Cast on 9 sts and work as foll: 1 selvage st, row 2 of eyelet panel over next 9 sts, p9, row 2 of eyelet panel over next 9 sts, 1 selvage st—29 sts.
Work 14 more rows in pat and rev St st, ending on row 16 of eyelet panel.
Next row Cast on 9 sts and work as foll: 1 selvage st, [k9 (for rev St st block), row 1 of eyelet panel over next 9 sts] twice, 1 selvage st—38 sts.
Next row Cast on 9 sts and work as foll: 1 selvage st, [p9, row 2 of eyelet panel over next 9 sts] twice, p9, 1 selvage st—47 sts.
Work 14 more rows in pat and rev St st, ending on row 16 of eyelet panel.
Cont to add panel blocks every 16 rows in this way, alternating rev St st and eyelet panel blocks, until center section is 23 blocks wide (209 sts), complete panels and end with a WS row.
*Bind off 9 sts at beg of next 2 rows, work 14 more rows to complete eyelet panels. Rep from * until final eyelet block is complete. Bind off rem 11 sts.

FINISHING
Block lightly to measurements.

Quenet

YOU'LL NEED

YARN: (3) 3½oz/100g, 250yd/230m of any DK weight wool blend yarn in ecru (A)

1¾oz/50g, 130yd/120m of any DK weight wool blend yarn in each light pink (C), aqua (D), blue (F), light blue (G), and dark rose (H)

1¾oz/50g, 130yd/120yd of any DK weight wool tweed yarn in rose (B) and green (E)

NEEDLES/HOOKS: One pair size 5 (3.75mm) needles *or size to obtain gauge*

Size B/1 (2.25mm) crochet hook

KNITTED MEASUREMENTS

• 22" x 26"/56cm x 66cm

GAUGE

23 sts and 27 rows to 4"/10cm over Fair Isle pat with size 5 (3.75mm) needles. *Take time to check gauge.*

Note

Carry yarn not in use *loosely* across back of work.

BLANKET

Fair Isle Squares (make 10 each from charts A and B)
With background shade (B or E), cast on 23 sts. Work in chart pat through row 23. Bind off.

Crochet Edging (Chart A squares)
Rnd 1 With RS of work facing and crochet hook, join B with sl st to any corner of square. Ch 1, work sc evenly around, working 3 sc in corners; join with C sl st to first sc. **Rnd 2** With C, ch 1, working in back loops only of each st, work sc evenly around, working 3 sc in corners; join H with sl st to first sc. **Rnd**

3 With H, rep rnd 2. **Rnd 4** With A, rep rnd 2.
Fasten off.

Crochet Edging (Chart B squares)
Work as for crochet edging of chart A squares using E, F, G and A.

FINISHING

Join Squares
Join squares into 4 strips, 5 squares long alternating square A with square B as shown. Place WS of squares tog, and with A, work 1 row of sc through both thicknesses to join tops and bottoms of squares to form strips 5 squares long. Join 4 strips tog in same way.

Crochet Border
Rnd 1 With RS facing and crochet hook, join A with sl st to bottom right corner of blanket, *work 117 sc to next corner, 3 sc in corner, 102 sc to next corner, 3 sc in corner; rep from * once more; join with sl st to first sc—450 sc.
Rnd 2 Ch 1, sc in first sc, *sk next 2 sc, 5 dc in next sc, sk next 2 sc, sc in next sc; rep from * around; join with sl st to first sc. Fasten off. Block blanket to measurements.

Chart A

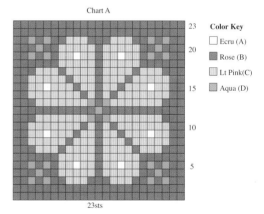

23
20
15
10
5

Color Key
☐ Ecru (A)
▨ Rose (B)
☐ Lt Pink(C)
▨ Aqua (D)

23sts

Chart B

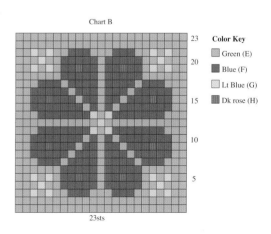

23
20
15
10
5

Color Key
☐ Green (E)
▨ Blue (F)
☐ Lt Blue (G)
▨ Dk rose (H)

23sts

Heirloom *SAMPLER*

YOU'LL NEED

YARN: 🔢 15¾oz/450g,1530yd/1430m of any sport weight wool yarn

NEEDLES/HOOKS: One pair size 3 (3.25mm) needles *or size to obtain gauge*

Size D/3 (3.25mm) crochet hook for square edging

ADDITIONAL: Cable needle

KNITTED MEASUREMENTS

• 28" x 37"/71cm x 94cm

GAUGE

25 sts and 34 rows to 4"/10cm over St st using size 3 (3.25mm) needles.
Take time to check gauge.

STITCH GLOSSARY

MB ([K1, yo] twice, k1) all in next st, slip 4th, 3rd, 2nd and first sts separately over 5th st; bobble complete.

6-st RC
Sl 3 sts to cn and hold to *back*, k3, k3 from cn.

Sl 5 wyif

H	F	E	B	G
B	A	D	C	F
H	G	E	D	A
D	H	F	A	G
A	G	E	B	C
F	C	G	H	B
A	B	C	D	E

35 Squares

Sl next 5 sts knitwise, one at a time, with yarn in front of work.

BLANKET

Square A (make 5)
Cast on 34 sts.
Row 1 (RS) Knit.
Row 2 K8, [p2, k6] 3 times, k2.
Row 3 P8, [k2, p6] 3 times, p2.
Row 4 Rep row 2.
Row 5 Knit.
Row 6 K4, [p2, k6] 3 times, p2, k4.
Row 7 P4, [k2, p6] 3 times, k2, p4.
Row 8 Rep row 6.
Rep rows 1-8 for basketweave pat until piece measures approx 5"/12.5cm ending with row 4 or 8 of pat. Bind off.

Square B (make 5)
Cast on 33 sts.
Row 1 (RS) Knit.
Row 2 and all WS rows Purl.
Row 3 K8, yo, sl 1, k2tog, psso, yo, k11, yo, sl 1, k2tog, psso, yo, k8.
Row 5 K6, k2tog, yo, k3, yo, ssk, k7, k2tog, yo, k3, yo, ssk, k6.
Row 7 K5, k2tog, yo, k5, yo, ssk, k5, k2tog, yo, k5, yo, ssk, k5.
Row 9 K4, k2tog, yo, k7, yo, ssk, k3, k2tog, yo, k7, yo, ssk, k4.
Row 11 K3, k2tog, yo, k9, yo, ssk, k1, k2tog, yo, k9, yo, ssk, k3.
Row 13 K2, k2tog, yo, k5, MB, k5, yo, sl 1, k2tog, psso, yo, k5, MB, k5, yo, ssk, k2.
Row 15 K4, yo, ssk, k7, k2tog, yo, k3, yo, ssk, k7, k2tog, yo, k4.
Row 17 [K5, yo, ssk, k5, k2tog, yo] twice, k5.
Row 19 K6, yo, ssk, k3, k2tog, yo, k7, yo, ssk, k3, k2tog, yo, k6.
Row 21 K7, yo, ssk, k1, k2tog, yo, k9, yo, ssk, k1, k2tog, yo, k7.
Row 23 K8, yo, sl 1, k2tog, psso, yo, k5, MB, k5, yo, sl 1, k2tog, psso, yo, k8.
Rows 25-44 Rep rows 5-22.
Row 45 Rep row 3.
Row 47 Knit.

Row 48 Purl.
Bind off.

Square C (make 4)
Cast on 36 sts.
Row 1 (RS) K2, p2, [k6, p2, k1, p2] twice, k6, p2, k2.
Row 2 and all WS rows K4, [p6, k5] twice, p6, k4.
Row 3 K2, p2, [6-st RC, p2, k1, p2] twice, 6-st RC, p2, k2.
Rows 5 and 7 Rep row 1.
Row 8 Rep row 2.
Rep rows 1-8 for cable pat until piece measures approx 5"/12.5cm ending with row 6 of pat. Bind off.

Square D (make 4)
Cast on 32 sts.
Row 1 (RS) K3, *k2tog, k5, yo, k1, yo, k2, ssk*, k2, rep from * to * once, k3.
Row 2 and all WS rows Purl.
Row 3 K3, *k2tog, k4, yo, k3, yo, k1, ssk*, k2, rep from * to * once, k3.
Row 5 K3, *k2tog, k3, yo, k5, yo, ssk*, k2, rep from * to * once, k3.
Row 7 K3, *k2tog, k2, yo, k1, yo, k5, ssk*, k2, rep from * to * once, k3.
Row 9 K3, *k2tog, k1, yo, k3, yo, k4, ssk*, k2, rep from * to * once, k3.
Row 11 K3, *k2tog, yo, k5, yo, k3, ssk*, k2, rep from * to * once, k3.
Row 12 Rep row 2.
Rep rows 1-12 for shell lace pat until square measures 5"/12.5cm ending with a WS row. Bind off.

Square E (make 4)
Cast on 34 sts.
Row 1 (WS) Purl.
Row 2 K1, [p1, k7] 4 times, k1.
Row 3 K1, [p6, k2] 4 times, k1.
Row 4 K1, [p3, k5] 4 times, k1.
Row 5 K1, [p4, k4] 4 times, k1.
Row 6 K1, [p5, k3] 4 times, k1.
Row 7 K1, [p2, k6] 4 times, k1.
Row 8 K1, [p7, k1] 4 times, k1.

Rep rows 1-8 for flag pat until piece measures approx 5"/12.5cm ending with row 1 of pat. Bind off.

Square F (make 4)
Cast on 35 sts.
Row 1 and all WS rows Purl.
Row 2 K3, *yo, ssk, k6; rep from * to end.
Row 4 K4, *yo, ssk, k3, k2tog, yo, k1; rep from * to last 7 sts, yo, ssk, k5.
Row 6 K5, *yo, ssk, k1, k2tog, yo, k3; rep from * to last 6 sts, yo, ssk, k4.

Row 8 K3, k2tog, *yo, k5, yo, sl 2 sts knitwise, k1, p2sso; rep from * to last 6 sts, yo, k6.
Row 10 K7, *yo, ssk, k6; rep from * to last 4 sts, yo, ssk, k2.
Row 12 K5, k2tog, *yo, k1, yo, ssk, k3, k2tog; rep from * to last 4 sts, yo, k4.
Row 14 K4, *k2tog, yo, k3, yo, ssk, k1; rep from * to last 7 sts, k2tog, yo, k5.
Row 16 K6, *yo, sl 2 sts knitwise, k1, p2sso, yo, k5; rep from * to last 5 sts, yo, k2tog, k3.
Rep rows 1-16 for rosebud lace pat until piece measures

approx 5"/12.5cm ending with row 1 or 9 of
pat. Bind off.

Square G (make 5)
Cast on 33 sts.
Row 1 (RS) K3, *yo, k2, p3, p3tog, p3, k2, yo,
k1; rep from * to last 2 sts, k2.
Row 2 P6, k7, p7, k7, p6.
Row 3 K3, *k1, yo, k2, p2, p3tog, p2, k2, yo,
k2; rep from * to last 2 sts, k2.
Row 4 P7, k5, p9, k5, p7.
Row 5 K5, *yo, k2, p1, p3tog, p1, k2, yo, k5;
rep from * to end.
Row 6 P8, k3, p11, k3, p8.
Row 7 K6, *yo, k2, p3tog, k2, yo, k7; rep from
*, end k6.
Row 8 P9, k1, p13, k1, p9.
Row 9 P2, p2tog, *p3, k2, yo, k1, yo, k2, p3 *,
p3tog, rep from * to * once, p2tog, p2.
Row 10 K2, *k4, p7, k3; rep from * to last 3
sts, k3.
Row 11 P2, p2tog, *p2, k2, yo, k3, yo, k2, p2 *, p3tog, rep from *
to * once, p2tog, p2.
Row 12 K2, *k3, p9, k2; rep from * to last 3 sts, k3.
Row 13 P2, p2tog, *p1, k2, yo, k5, yo, k2, p1*, p3tog, rep from *
to * once, p2tog, p2.
Row 14 K2, *k2, p11, k1; rep from * to last 3 sts, k3.
Row 15 P2, p2tog. *k2, yo, k7, yo, k2*, p3tog, rep from * to *
once, p2tog, p2.
Row 16 K2, *k1, p13; rep from * to last 3 sts, k3.
Rep rows 1-16 for wave pat until piece measures approx
5"/12.5cm ending with row 8 or 16 of pat. Bind off.

Square H (make 4)
Cast on 29 sts.
Row 1 (RS) Knit.
Rows 2, 4 and 6 Purl.
Rows 3, 5 and 7 K2, *k5, sl 5 wyif; rep from * to last 7 sts, k7.
Row 8 P9, *with RH needle in front of work, insert needle under
3 loose strands (from bottom to top) and p these 3 strands tog,
p1, pass the p3tog over p1, p9; rep from * to end.
Rows 9, 11 and 13 K2, *sl 5 wyif, k5; rep from * to last 7 sts, sl
5 wyif, k2.
Rows 10 and 12 Purl.
Row 14 P4, *insert RH needle under 3 loose strands on RS of
work, yo and draw up a lp, purl next st and sl lp just made over
purl st, p9; rep from *, end last rep with p4.
Rep rows 3-14 three times more for bow-tie pat.
Next row Knit.
Next row Purl.
Bind off.

Quenet

FINISHING

With crochet hook, join yarn with sl st in any corner and work
sc evenly around outer edge of each square, working 3 sc in
corners; join with sl st to first sc. Fasten off.
Sew squares together as shown in diagram.

Lace Edging
Cast on 11 sts.
Row 1 (RS) Sl 1, k1 tbl, yo, k1, [yo, ssk] 3 times, k2.
Row 2 and all WS rows Purl.
Row 3 Sl 1, k1 tbl, yo, k3, [yo, ssk] 3 times, k1.
Row 5 Sl 1, k1 tbl, yo, k5, [yo, ssk] twice, k2.
Row 7 Sl 1, k1 tbl, yo, k7, [yo, ssk] twice, k1.
Row 9 Ssk, k1, yo, ssk, k3, [k2tog, yo] twice, k3.
Row 11 Ssk, k1, yo, ssk, k1, [k2tog, yo] 3 times, k2.
Row 13 Ssk, k1, yo, sl 1, k2tog, psso, (yo, k2tog) twice, yo, k3.
Row 15 Ssk, k2, [k2tog, yo] 3 times, k2.
Row 16 Purl.
Rep rows 1-16 for lace edging pat until piece measures length to
fit around outer edge of blanket (approx 135"/343cm) ending
with row 16 of pat. Bind off. Sew straight side of edging to
blanket, gathering slightly at corners. Sew cast-on and bound-off
edges tog.

Block to measurements.

Octagonal LACE

YOU'LL NEED

YARN:  **1** 8¾oz/250g, 1000yd/930m of any fingering weight wool

NEEDLES/HOOKS: 1 set (5) size 4 (3.5mm) dpns *or size to obtain gauge*

Size B/1 (2mm) crochet hook

KNITTED MEASUREMENTS

• 32" x 28"/81cm x 71cm

GAUGE

One octagonal medallion measures 6½"/ 16.5cm and one seed st square measures 2"/5cm.
Take time to check gauge.

MEDALLION (make 18)

Note
Medallions are knit in rnds and divided onto 4 needles. To make working the first few rnds easier, divide sts on 3 needles then transfer to 4 when there are enough sts to work comfortably.
Cast on 8 sts evenly divided onto 3 needles. Join to work in rnds.
Rnd 1 K1 tbl in each st around.
Rnd 2 [Yo, k1] 8 times.
Rnd 3 and all odd rnds Knit.
Change to 4 dpns while working next rnd.
Rnd 4 [Yo, k2] 8 times.
Rnd 6 [Yo, k3] 8 times.
Rnd 8 [Yo, k4] 8 times.
Rnd 10 [Yo, k5] 8 times.
Rnd 12 [Yo, k6] 8 times.
Rnd 14 [Yo, k7] 8 times.
Rnd 16 [Yo, k8] 8 times.
Rnd 18 [Yo, k1, yo, k2tog, k6] 8 times.
Rnd 20 *Yo, k1, [yo, k2tog] twice, k5; rep from * 7 times more.
Rnd 22 *Yo, k1, [yo, k2tog] 3 times, k4; rep from * 7 times more.
Rnd 24 *Yo, k1, [yo, k2tog] 4 times, k3; rep from * 7 times more.
Rnd 26 *Yo, k1, [yo, k2tog] 5 times, k2; rep from * 7 times more.
Rnd 28 *Yo, k1, [yo, k2tog] 6 times, k1;

rep from * 7 times more.
Rnd 30 *Yo, k1, [yo, k2tog] 7 times; rep from * 7 times more.
Bind off all sts on next rnd.

SQUARE

Note
Squares are worked on 17 of the 18 medallions by picking up and knitting 17 sts along one of the straight edges. This eliminates the sewing of one edge.
With one dpn, pick up and k 17 sts in back lps only along one straight edge of medallion. Work back and forth with 2 needles as foll:
Rows 1-7 *K1, p1; rep from *, end k1 (for seed st).
Row 8 (RS) Work 8 sts in seed st, in next st, work 1 bobble as foll: K1, k1 tbl, k1, k1 tbl, k1 in same st for 5 sts, turn; k5; turn; p5; turn, pass the 4th, 3rd, 2nd and 1st st over the last st; work 8 sts in seed st.
Row 9 and all odd rows Work even in seed st.
Row 10 Work 6 sts in seed st, work 1 bobble, 3 sts in seed st, work 1 bobble, 6 sts in seed st.
Row 12 Rep row 8.

Row 14 Rep row 10.
Row 16 Rep row 8.
Rows 18-24 Work even in seed st. Bind off in seed st.

FINISHING

Block pieces evenly. Using diagram, lay out pieces and assemble by sewing tog through back lps on RS with an overcast st. With crochet hook, work an edge of sc around entire outer edge working (sc, ch 1, sc) in each outer center.

Quenet

PLACEMENT DIAGRAM

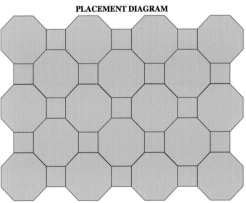

Counting SHEEP

Quenet

KNITTED MEASUREMENTS

• 27" x 37"/68.5cm x 94cm

GAUGE

21 sts and 28 rows to 4"/10cm over rev St st using size 6 (4mm) needles.
Take time to check gauge.

STITCH GLOSSARY

Moss Stitch (even number of sts)
Rows 1 and 2 *K1, p1; rep from * to end.
Rows 3 and 4 *P1, k1; rep from * to end.
Rep rows 1-4 for moss st.
Inc 2 On WS, k1, p1 and k1 in one st.
Make Ear Cast on 4 sts using 2-needle cast-on as foll: [K1, do not drop st from LH needle, place st just made on LH needle] 4 times. Bind off 4 sts.

BLANKET

Cast on 142 sts. Work back and forth in moss st for 14 rows, end with a WS row.

Next row (RS) Work moss st over 10 sts, rev St st over 122 sts, moss st over 10 sts.
Cont in pat as established for 17 more rows.

Beg lamb charts
Row 1 Work moss st over 10 sts, rev St st over 27 sts, lamb chart over 20 sts, rev St st over 23 sts, lamb chart over 20 sts, rev St st over 32 sts, moss st over 10 sts. Cont in pat as

established for 17 more rows.
Row 19 Work moss st over 10 sts, rev St st over 122 sts, moss st over 10 sts. Cont in pat as established for 25 rows more.
Row 45 Work moss st over 10 sts, rev St st over 6 sts, [lamb chart over 20 sts, rev St st over 23 sts] twice, lamb chart over 20 sts, rev St st over 10 sts, moss st over 10 sts. Cont in pat as established for 17 more rows.
Rows 63-88 Rep rows 19-44. Rep rows 1-88 once more, then rows 1-18 once more.
Next row (RS) Work moss st over 10 sts, rev St st over 122 sts, moss st over 10 sts.
Cont in pat as established for 17 more rows. Work all sts in moss st for 14 rows. Bind off in pat.

FINISHING

Block to measurements.

LAMB CHART

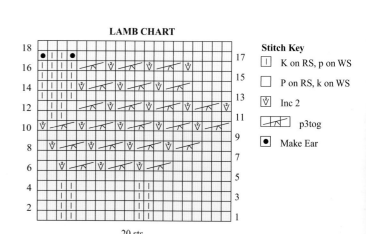

Stitch Key
- ☐ K on RS, p on WS
- ☐ P on RS, k on WS
- Ⅴ Inc 2
- ⟋⟍ p3tog
- ● Make Ear

20 sts

Sweet SAFARI

YOU'LL NEED

YARN:  8¾oz/250g, 550yd/ 500m of any DK weight cotton in blue (A)

7oz/200g, 440yd/400m in yellow (B)

1¾oz/50g, 110yd/100m in brown (C)

NEEDLES: One pair size 6 (4mm) needles *or size to obtain gauge.*

ADDITIONAL: Size 6 steel (1.5mm) crochet hook , bobbins

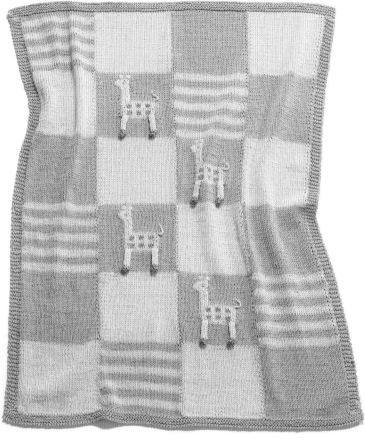

Quenet

KNITTED MEASUREMENTS

• 27½" x 34"/70cm x 86.5cm

GAUGE

20 sts and 27 rows to 4"/10 cm over St st using size 6 (4mm) needles.
Take time to check gauge.

BLOCKS

Yellow [Blue] Block (make 9 [6])
32 sts and 36 rows with B [A].

Stripe Block 1 (make 2)
32 sts as foll: [4 rows A, 4 rows B] 4 times, 4 rows A.

Stripe Block 2 (make 3)
32 sts as foll: [4 rows B, 4 rows A] 4 times, 4 rows B.

Giraffe Block (make 4)
32 sts as foll: **Row 1-10** St st with A. **Rows 11-33** Work 23 rows giraffe chart as foll: **Next row (RS)** 7 sts A, 17 sts chart, 8 sts A. **Rows 34-36** St st with A.

BLANKET

With A, cast on 138 sts. Work in garter st for 1"/2.5cm. **Next row (RS)** Cont 5 sts garter st with A, work blocks St st as foll: blue, yellow, stripe 1, yellow, cont last 5 sts in garter st with A. Cont as established, foll photo for placement, until all blocks have been worked. With A, work in garter st over all sts for 1"/2.5cm. Bind off.

FINISHING

Block piece to measurements. Embroider eyes of giraffe with A and French knot.

Giraffe legs

With C, cast on 6 sts for hoof. Work in garter st for 3 rows. Join B and work in St st for 9 rows. Bind off. Fold piece lengthwise and sew back seam and bottom of hoof tog. With seam at back, sew legs to giraffe.

Giraffe tail

Separate 3 strands of B. Using crochet hook, ch 10. Fasten off. Attach to giraffe.

Giraffe horn

Separate 2 strands B. Using crochet hook, ch 10. Fasten off and form a circle. Sew to top of ears.

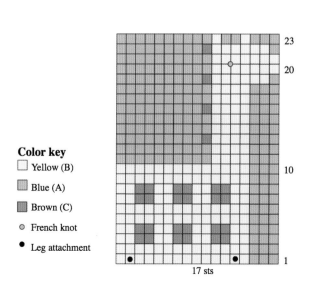

Color key
☐ Yellow (B)
▨ Blue (A)
▨ Brown (C)
○ French knot
● Leg attachment

17 sts

Mitered Square THROW

YOU'LL NEED

YARN:  2 3½oz/100g balls (each approx 207yd/188m) of Lion Brand Yarn Company Cotton Ease (cotton/acrylic) each in candy blue (A), mint (B), pistachio (C), ice blue (D) and sugar plum (E))

NEEDLES: One pair each size 6 (4mm) and size 9 (5.5mm) needles *or size to obtain gauge*

KNITTED MEASUREMENTS

• 42" x 42"/106.5cm x 106.5cm

GAUGE

16 sts and 22 rows to 4"/10cm over St st using size 9 (5.5mm) needles.
Take time to check gauge.

Note

Blanket is worked in rounds, starting at center. Each square is picked up from the squares worked before it. Follow diagram for color placement. All squares on outer edges of Blanket have 2 sts at each edge worked in garter st.

STITCH GLOSSARY

CDD (centered double decrease)
Slip next 2 sts tog as if to k2tog, then knit next st; using tip of LH needle, pass 2 slipped sts over last knit st.

BLANKET

Square 1

With smaller needles and first color, cast on 29 sts. K 1 row. Change to larger needles.
Row 1 K13, CDD, k to end.
Row 2 and all WS rows Purl.
Row 3 K12, CDD, k to end.
Row 5 K11, CDD, k to end.
Cont as established, working one fewer st before dec each row until 13 sts rem, end with RS facing. Cut first color. Change to second color and cont working established decs until 3 sts rem.
Next row (WS) Sl first 2 sts purlwise, p1, pass 2 slipped sts over last purl st. Fasten off.

Square 2

With smaller needles and first color, pick up and k 14 sts along edge of previous square, 1 st in top CDD of square, then cast on 14 sts—29 sts. Complete as for square 1.

Color Key
- Candy blue (A)
- Mint (B)
- Pistachio (C)
- Ice blue (D)
- Sugar plum (E)

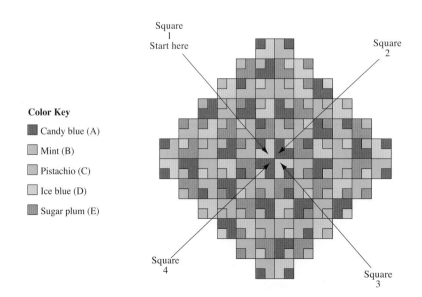

Square 3

With smaller needles and first color, cast on 14 sts, pick up 1 st in top CDD of square below, then pick up and k 14 sts along edge of previous square—29 sts.

Complete as for square 1.

Square 4

With smaller needles and first color, pick up and k 14 sts along edge of previous square, 1 st in top CDD of square below and 14 sts along edge of next previous square—29 sts.

Complete as for square 1.

Foll diagram for color placement, work all squares beg with square 1 and picking up all foll squares from previously worked ones.

Squares on outer edges

Work as for square 4, noting all WS rows will be worked as foll: k2, purl to last 2 sts, k2.

FINISHING

Block lightly to measurements.

Lincoln LOGS

Rose Callahan

YOU'LL NEED

YARN: 🔵4 *Cotton-Ease* by Lion Brand Co., 3½oz/100g, 207yd/188m cotton and acrylic blend

1 ball each in #186 maize (A), #134 terracotta (B), #110 lake (C) and #191 violet (F)

2 balls each in #112 berry (D) and #194 lime (E)

NEEDLES: Size 8 (5mm) needles *or size to obtain gauge*

KNITTED MEASUREMENTS
• 36"x 29"/91.5cm x 73.5cm

GAUGE
18 sts and 36 rows to 4"/10cm over garter st using size 8 (5mm) needles.
Take time to check gauge.

BLOCK (make 12)
With A, cast on 8 sts. Working all rows as foll: Sl 1 purlwise

PLACEMENT DIAGRAM

COLOR KEY
☐ Maize (A)
■ Terra Cotta (B)
▨ Lake (C)
▨ Berry (D)
☐ Lime (E)

⬅ = Direction of work

wyib, k to end, work 14 rows. Change to B and work 14 rows. Bind off all sts, leaving last loop on needle. Turn piece counter-clockwise 90°, pick up and knit 14 sts. Work 13 rows, change to C and work 14 rows. Bind off all sts, cut yarn and fasten off. Turn work 90° clockwise, attach yarn at right corner, pick up and knit 22 sts. Work 13 rows, change to D and work 14 rows. Bind off all sts, leaving last loop on needle.
Turn work counter-clockwise 90°, pick up and knit 28 sts. Work 13 rows, change to E and work 14 rows. Bind off all sts, cut yarn and fasten off. Turn work 90° clockwise, attach yarn at right corner, pick up and knit 36 sts. Work 13 rows, bind off all sts.

FINISHING
Using photo for reference, lay pieces in a 3 x 4 grid. With E, join pieces.

Border
With F, pick up and knit 106 sts along one short end of rectangle. Work 13 rows, bind off. Rep for other short end. With F, pick up and knit 155 sts along one long side. Work 13 rows, bind off. Rep for other long side.

Mistral THROW

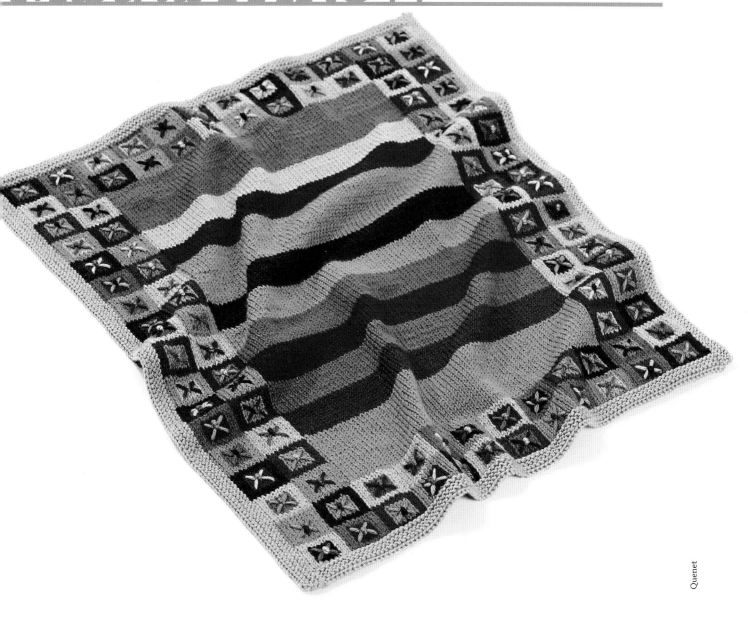

Quenet

YOU'LL NEED

YARN: 🧶**4** 3½oz/100g, 170yd/160m of any worsted weight wool in oatmeal (A)

1¾oz/50g, 85yd/80m in amethyst (B), thyme (C), nectar (orange) (D), russet (red) (E), dijon (F), cornflower blue (G), raisin (burgundy) (H), damson (purple) (J), and mist (teal) (L)

NEEDLES: One pair each sizes 7 and 8 (4.5 and 5mm) needles *or size to obtain gauge.*

ADDITIONAL: Tapestry needle

KNITTED MEASUREMENTS

• 26" x 31½"/66cm x 80cm

GAUGE

18 sts and 24 rows to 4"/10 cm over St st using larger needles.
Take time to check gauge.

STRIPE PATTERN

10 rows each B, D, L, E, F, G, J, C, D, E, B, H, G and C.

Mistral THROW

CHART 1–Left Half

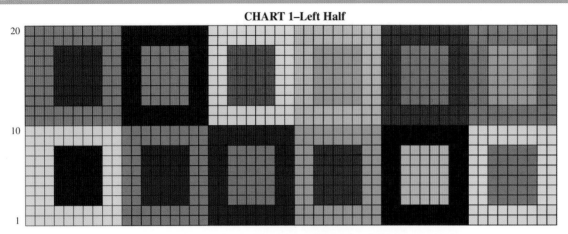

CHART 1–Right Half

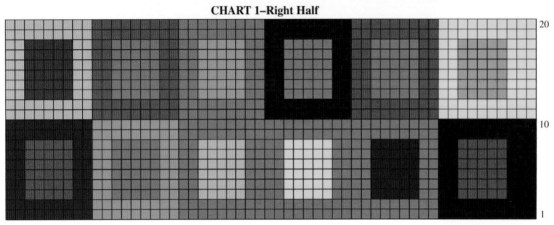

CHART 4–Left Half

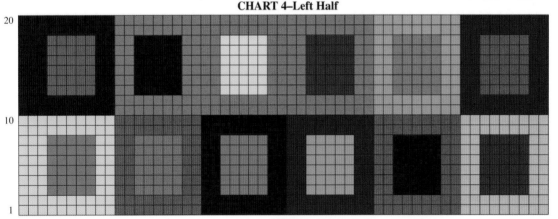

110 sts

CHART 4–Right Half

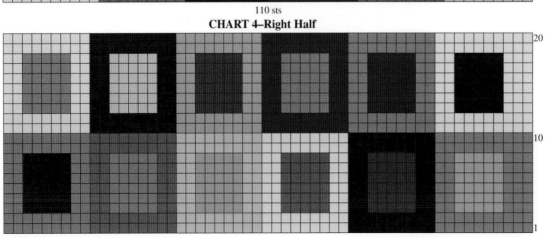

Color key

- Oatmeal (A)
- Amethyst (B)
- Thyme (C)
- Nectar (D)
- Russet (E)
- Dijon (F)
- Cornflower (G)
- Raisin (H)
- Damson (J)
- Mist (L)

PAGE 36

BLANKET

With smaller needles and A, cast on 110 sts. Work in garter st for 6 rows. Change to larger needles. Work in St st and charts as foll: Work 20 rows chart 1.

Next row (RS) Work 19 sts chart 2, 72 sts stripe pat, 19 sts chart 3. Cont in pats as established until 140 rows of stripe pat have been worked. Work 20 rows chart 4. Change to smaller needles and A. Work in garter st for 6 rows. Bind off knitwise.

Side Borders

With RS facing, smaller needles and A, pick up and k 144 sts evenly along one side edge. Work in garter st for 5 rows. Bind off knitwise. Work in same way along other side edge.

FINISHING

Block to measurements.

With tapestry needle work large cross sts in center of all small squares in a contrast color. Anchor crosses with a 3-wrap French knot using another color.

CHART 3

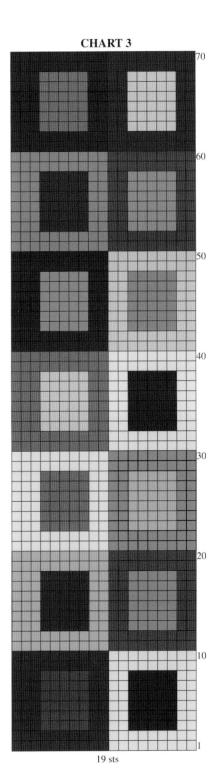

19 sts

CHART 2

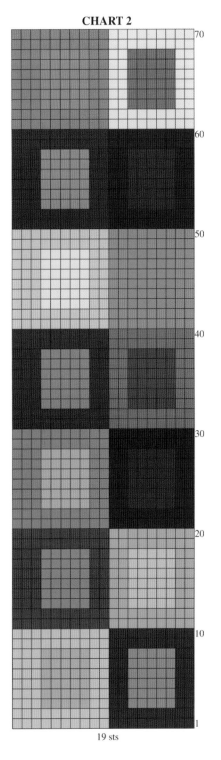

19 sts

Felted BLANKET

Quenet

YOU'LL NEED

YARN:  8¾oz/250g,
540yd/500m of any variegated
worsted weight wool in self-striping
pinks (A) and greens (B)

NEEDLES: One size 6 (4mm)
circular needle 36"/90cm long *or size
to obtain gauge*

KNITTED MEASUREMENTS

- 37" x 43"/94cm x 109cm
  (before felting)
- 27" x 32"/68.5cm x 81.5cm
  (after felting)

GAUGE

14 sts to 4"/10cm over St st using
size 6(4mm) needle (before felting).
Take time to check gauge.

STITCH GLOSSARY

Seed Stitch
Row 1 (RS) *K1, p1; rep from * to end.
Row 2 *P1, k1; rep from * to end.
Rep last 2 rows for seed st.
Stripe Pat
Row 1 (RS) With B, work 6 sts in seed st, k to last 6 sts, work 6
sts in seed st.
Row 2 Work 6 sts in seed st, p to last 6 sts, work 6 sts in seed st.
Rows 3 and 4 Rep last 2 rows once.
Rows 5 to 8 With A, rep last 4 rows once.
Rep last 8 rows for stripe pat.

Note
Carry yarn up side of work when working stripes.

BLANKET

With A, cast on 130 sts.
Working back and forth in rows, work 6 rows in seed st.
Work in stripe pat until piece measures approx 42"/106.5cm
from beg, end with 8th row of stripe pat.
With B, work 6 rows in seed st. Bind off.

FINISHING

Felting
Weave in all yarn ends. Set your washing machine at lowest
water level (enough to just cover blanket), hottest temperature
and highest agitation. Add blanket and small amount of liquid
detergent. Begin washing and check on blanket approx every
5 minutes until desired felting of fabric is achieved; the stitch
definition should be almost unrecognizable. Remove blanket
and rinse by hand in lukewarm water. Roll blanket in towels to
remove excess water. Dry flat.

Textured BLANKET

Quenet

YOU'LL NEED

YARN:  14oz/400g, 1220yd/
1120m of any worsted weight wool yarn

NEEDLES: Size 7 (4.5mm) circular
needle 29"/74cm long *or size to obtain
gauge*

ADDITIONAL: Cable needle (cn)

KNITTED MEASUREMENTS
• 32" x 32"/81.5 x 81.5cm

GAUGE
26 sts and 28 rows to 4"/10cm over cable pat using size 7
(4.5mm) needles.
Take time to check gauge.

STITCH GLOSSARY
Right twist (RT) Pass in front of first st and k 2nd st,

then k first st and let both sts fall from needle.
6-st RPC Sl next 3 sts to cn and hold to *back*, k1, p1, k1,
then from cn work k1, p1, k1.
Cable Pattern
Row 1 (RS) [K1, p1, k1, p2, k1, p1, RT, p1, k1, p2] 16
times, k1, p1, k1.
Row 2 and all WS rows [K1, p1, k1, RT, p1, k1, p2, k1,
p1, RT] 16 times, k1, p1, k1.
Row 3 [K1, p1, k1, p2, 6-st RPC, p2, k1, p1, k1, p2, k1, p1,
RT, p1, k1, p2] 8 times, k1, p1, k1.
Rows 5 and 7 Rep row 1.
Row 9 [K1, p1, k1, p2, k1, p1, RT, p1, k1, p2, k1, p1, k1,
p2, 6-st RPC, p2] 8 times, k1, p1, k1.
Row 11 Rep row 1.
Row 12 Rep row 2.
Rep rows 1-12 for cable pat.

BLANKET
Cast on 211 sts. Work in cable pat until piece measures
32"/81.5cm, end with a WS row. Bind off.

FINISHING
Lightly block blanket to measurements.

Diamond THROW

YOU'LL NEED

YARN:  3½oz/100g, 250yd/230m of any DK weight cotton in beige (MC)

1¾oz/50g, 125yd/115m in blue/grey (A), lt green (B), rust (C), brown (D), pink (E), cream (F), lt brown (G), and lilac (H)

1¾oz/50g, 180yd/160m of any worsted weight cotton chenille in cream (I), green (J), and tan (K)

1¾oz/50g, 190yd/170m of any fingering weight cotton in beige (M) and brown (L)

NEEDLES: One pair size 4 (3.5mm) needles *or size to obtain gauge*

ADDITIONAL: Size E/4 (3.5mm) crochet hook, bobbins

KNITTED MEASUREMENTS

• 23" x 26"/58.5cm x 66cm

GAUGE

24 sts and 34 rows to 4"/10cm over St st using size 4 (3.5mm) needles.
Take time to check gauge.

Note

When changing colors, twist yarns on WS to prevent holes in work. Use a separate bobbin of yarn for each block of color.

BLANKET

With MC, cast on 132 sts. K 2 rows.
Beg chart pat
Next row (RS) K3 MC, work 72-st rep of chart once, then work first 54 sts once

more, k3 MC. Cont in pats as established, keeping first and last 3 sts in garter st with MC, through chart row ___, then cont to work squares alternating solid blocks with striped blocks (each block is 18 sts and 18 rows) in colors as desired (use photo for inspiration) until 11 rows of blocks (or 198 rows). then work rows 1-90 once more. With MC, k 2 rows. Bind off.

FINISHING

Block to measurements.

Picot edging
Rnd 1 With RS facing, crochet hook and MC, work 1 rnd sc evenly around outside edge of throw.
Rnd 2 Sl st in first st, *ch 3, 1 dc in next st, sl st in next st; rep from * around. Join with sl st to first picot and fasten off.

Quenet

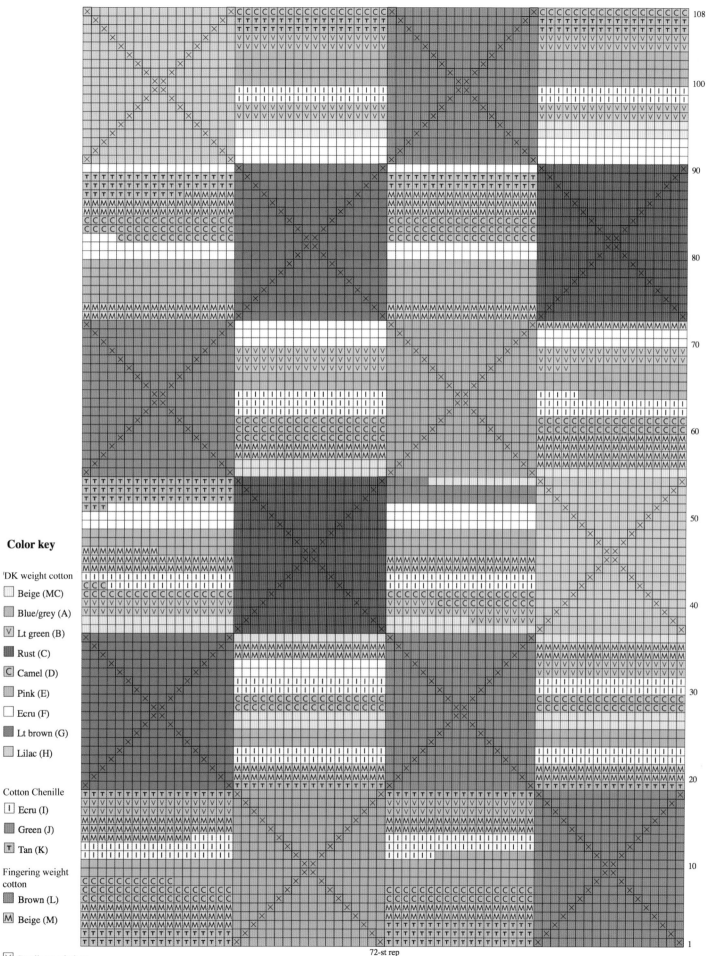

Color key

DK weight cotton
- ☐ Beige (MC)
- ▨ Blue/grey (A)
- Ⅴ Lt green (B)
- ■ Rust (C)
- Ⅽ Camel (D)
- ▦ Pink (E)
- ☐ Ecru (F)
- ▩ Lt brown (G)
- ▥ Lilac (H)

Cotton Chenille
- Ⅰ Ecru (I)
- ▦ Green (J)
- Ⅰ Tan (K)

Fingering weight cotton
- ▩ Brown (L)
- Ⅿ Beige (M)

☒ Duplicate stitch in
any contrasting color

72-st rep

Cute CRITTERS

Quenet

YOU'LL NEED

YARN: 🔳 **3** 7oz/200g, 530yd/480m of any DK weight wool yarn in cream (A)

3½oz/50g, 131yd/118m of any DK weight wool yarn in each dk blue (B), lt blue (C), dk green (D) and lt green (E)

1¾oz/50g, 131yd/118m of any DK weight wool yarn ball in yellow (C)

NEEDLES/HOOKS: One pair each sizes 7 and 8 (4.5 and 5mm) needles *or size to obtain gauge*

Size F/5 (4mm) crochet hook

KNITTED MEASUREMENTS

• 32" x 39"/81cm x 99cm

GAUGE

18 sts and 33 1/3 rows to 4"/10cm over garter st using larger needles.
Take time to check gauge

Note

Each row of chart squares represents 2 rows (RS and WS) of knitting. Pick-up row is row 1 of chart.

SOLID SQUARES

With larger needles and B, beg with lower left square on diagram, cast on 20 sts. P 40 rows. Leave sts on needle. Make 4 more squares in the same way. See diagram for color placement. At the end of the last (5th) square, bind off 20 sts. Turn, holding completed squares on LH needle.

ANIMAL SQUARES

With RS facing larger needles and A, pick up and k 20 sts along left side of the 5th solid square. Turn and k20 (row 2 of chart). Cont to foll chart for animal pat and work as foll:
Row 1 K19, k last st of animal square tog with first st of 4th solid square. Turn.
Row 2 K20. Turn.
Rep last 2 rows until all 40 rows of chart have been worked. Do not cut A.
With A, pick up and k 20 sts along left side of 4th solid square and work as for first animal square. Cont in this way until 4 animal squares have been worked. Leave all sts on RH needle.
Second row of solid squares
With E, cast on 20 sts onto LH needle.
Next row (RS) P20. Turn.
Next row P19, p last st tog with first st from next animal

BEAR

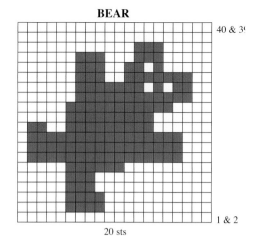

40 & 39

1 & 2

20 sts

BUNNY

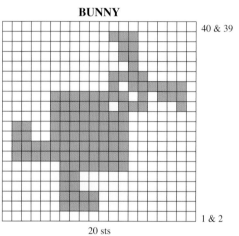

40 & 39

1 & 2

20 sts

BUTTERFLY

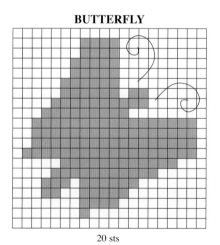

20 sts

FISH

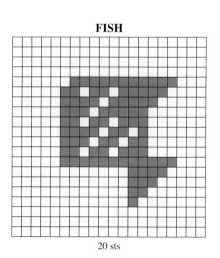

20 sts

square. Turn. Rep last 2 rows until 40 rows have been worked. Cut yarn.

With WS facing and B, pick up and p 20 sts along left side of next animal square. Complete square as before. Work 3 more solid squares in same way, leaving sts on RH needle. At end of the 5th square, bind off 20 sts. Turn and work a row of animal squares. Cont in this way to alternate solid squares with animal squares until there are 6 rows of solid squares and 5 rows of animal squares. On the last row of solid squares, bind off 20 sts at the end of each square.

FINISHING

Embroider antenna on butterfly with stem st.

Border

With smaller needles and A, cast on 2 sts. **Row 1** Knit. **Row 2** K1, M1, k1. **Row 3** K3. **Row 4** K1, M1, k2. **Row 5** K5. **Row 6** K1, M1, k3. **Rows 7-9** K5. **Row 10** K1, k2tog, k2. **Row 11** K4. **Row 12** K1, k2tog, k1. **Row 13** K3. **Row 14** K1, k2tog. Rep rows 1-14 for 101 times more. Bind off rem 2 sts. With RS of afghan facing, pin trim to edges with points toward the outside. Place 2 points along the edge of each solid square and curve one point at the outside corner of each solid square.

Attach border to afghan as foll: With crochet hook and A, working from WS, work 1 sc through trim and afghan, working 1 st in every other row (between each garter ridge) and in each cast-on and bound-off st. Block border.

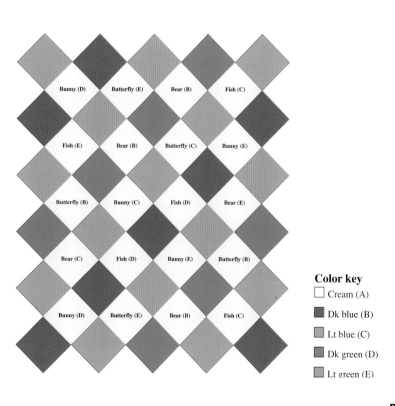

Color key

☐ Cream (A)

■ Dk blue (B)

■ Lt blue (C)

■ Dk green (D)

■ Lt green (E)

Patchwork PERFECTION

Quenet

Quenet

YOU'LL NEED

YARN: 〔2〕 7oz/200g, 540yd/500m of any sport weight wool blend yarn in grey (A)

3½oz/100g, 270yd/250m in peach (C) and aqua (D)

1¾oz/50g, 135yd/125m in camel (B) and mauve (E)

NEEDLES: One pair size 4 (3.5mm) needles *or size to obtain gauge*

Size 2 (2.5mm) circular needle, 29"/74cm long

KNITTED MEASUREMENTS

• 26½"/67cm x 26½"/67cm square

GAUGE

26 sts and 52 rows to 4"/10cm over garter st using size 4 (3.5mm) needles
One pinwheel quadrant is 2½"/6.5cm square.
Take time to check gauge.

Notes

1. There is a total of 16 quilt squares, each formed by putting together four matching color quadrants in positions to form a pinwheel design (see layout diagram).
2. The lattice strips, in colors C and D, are worked by picking up sts along the sides of the squares in the numerical order (1-15) and knit in the direction as shown in the layout diagram.

BLANKET

Quadrant (make 12 in each colorway)
With A, cast on 1 st.
Row 1 K1.
Row 2 (WS) K1 into front, back and front of st.
Row 3 K3.
Row 4 K1 into front and back of first st, k1, k1 into front and back of last st.
Row 5 K5.
Row 6 K1 into front and back of first st, k to last st, k1 into front and back of last st.
Row 7 and all odd rows Knit.
Rows 8, 10, 12, 14, 16, 18 and 20 Rep row 6—21 sts.

Row 21 With A, knit. Cut A. Work rem of quadrant with B, C, D or E.
Row 22 (WS) With B, C, D or E, SKP, k to last 2 sts, k2tog—19 sts.
Row 23 and all odd rows With working contrast color, knit.
Rows 24, 26, 28, 20, 32, 34, 34, 36 and 38 With working contrast color, rep row 22—3 sts.
Last row SK2P. Fasten off.

Square
Foll layout diagram for colors, sew tog 4 quadrants positioned to form the square as shown in layout diagram. Work lattice strips as foll:

Strip 1
With D, pick up and k 30 sts along side of first lower left square as in diagram. K18 rows. Bind off. Join this D pinwheel square to next B pinwheel square by sewing this piece along strip from RS.

Strip 2
With C, pick up and k 30 sts along lower edge of D square and k18 rows in the direction shown. Bind off. Join this D pinwheel square to next E pinwheel square by sewing from RS.

Strip 3
With D, pick up and k 69 sts along the 2 joined side squares and k 18 rows in the direction shown. Bind off.

Strip 4
With C, pick up and k 69 sts along the 2 joined lower squares and k 18 rows in this direction. Bind off.

Strip 5
With D, pick up and k 30 sts along the top square and k 18 rows in the direction shown. Bind off. Sew to side of next top square.

Strip 6
With C, pick up and k 69 sts along the 2 joined squares and k 18 rows in this direction. Bind off.

Strip 7
Sew squares into position, then with D, pick up and k 69 sts along the joined squares and k 18 rows in this direction. Bind off. Cont to work strips in this way, sewing squares tog when necessary, working short strips 8, 10 and 14 with 30 sts in colors as in diagram and strips 9, 11, 12, 13 and 15 with 69 sts in colors as in diagram. Finish by sewing any open ends of squares and strips tog.

FINISHING
Block to measurements.

Outside edge
With C, from RS and circular needle, pick up and k sts along one edge of square as foll: 29 sts along one square, [9 sts along lattice strip, 29 sts along one square] twice —105 sts. Slide sts to opposite end of needle and rejoin C to work first row from RS.
Row 1 (RS) With C, knit.
Row 2 With C, k1 into front and back of first st, (for inc) k to last st, inc 1 st in last st.
Row 3 K1C, *k2D, k2C; rep from * to end.
Row 4 Inc 1C st, *p2C, p2D; rep from *, end inc 1 C st in last st. Cut yarn leaving long ends.
Row 5 (RS) With A, knit.
Row 6 With A, inc 1 st in first st, k to last st, inc 1 st in last st.
Rows 7, 9 and 11 Rep row 5.
Rows 8 and 10 Rep row 6.
Bind off knitwise with A. Using 2 strands C, whip st corners of edging tog as in photo.

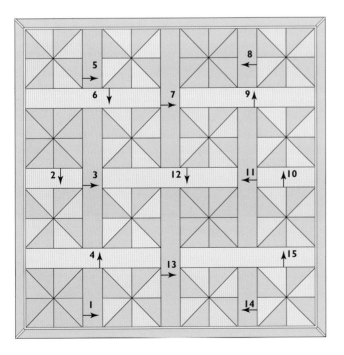

Color Key
☐ Grey (A)
☐ Camel (B)
☐ Peach (C)
☐ Aqua (D)
☐ Mauve (E)
← Indicates direction of work

Barn DANCE

Jose Santa

YOU'LL NEED

YARN:  10½oz/300g, 770yd/710m of any DK weight cotton in blue (A)

7oz/200g, 520yd/470m in pink (B) and green (D)

3½oz/100g, 260yd/236m in yellow (C), black (E), and white (F)

NEEDLES: Size 6 (4mm) circular needle, 40"/101.5cm long *or size to obtain gauge*

KNITTED MEASUREMENTS

• 32 x 36"/81 x 91.5cm

GAUGE

20 sts and 24 rows to 4"/10cm over St st using size 6 (4mm) needle.
Take time to check gauge

STRIPE PATTERN

*In St st, work 4 rows B, 4 rows D; rep from *.

Notes

1. Border: For the entire length of blanket, the first and last 5 sts are worked with D in garter st. The body of the blanket is worked in St st.
2. Each square is 28 sts and 34 rows.
3. The number on the placement diagram within the animal represents the chart # to be knit in that position.
4. The squares may be knit separately, if desired, and sewn together using the placement diagram.
5. To avoid holes, twist yarns when changing colors.
6. Body of lamb is worked in seed st.

BLANKET

With D, cast on 158 sts. Work in garter st for 8 rows.
Next row (RS) Work border as described in note 1, *k28 sts A (square), 2 sts D (inside border); rep from * 3 times more, end with 28 st A work border—5 squares, with 4 inside borders have been established. Cont as established for 5 rows.

Beg charts
Cont working squares and inside borders as established, AT SAME TIME, work charts as noted on diagram, centered within each square.
Work through 34 rows.
Next row (RS) Work 2 rows D (sts 6-34 and sts 124-152 form side borders).
Next row (RS) Work border, k28 sts A (side square), 92 sts D, 28 sts A (side square), work border.
Work even for 1 row.
Next row (RS) Work border, k28 sts A, beg stripe pat over next 92 sts, work 28 sts A, work border. Cont as established for 7 rows.

Beg charts
Cont in pats as established, AT SAME TIME, work charts as noted on diagram, centered within each square. Cont working until all side squares are completed and stripe pat ends with 4 rows B. Work 2 rows D.

Next row (RS) Establish squares and inside borders as for bottom squares, using diagram for placement of charts. Work through row 34 rows. With D work 8 rows garter st. Bind off.

FINISHING
Block lightly.

Lamb
Ears
With E, form 8-st chain lp, sew the center of lp tog and tack down. Foll chart and photo for placement.

Eyes
With A, work french knot, foll chart and photo for placement.

Pig
Ears
With B, form 7-st chain lp, sew the center of lp tog and tack down. Foll chart and photo for placement.

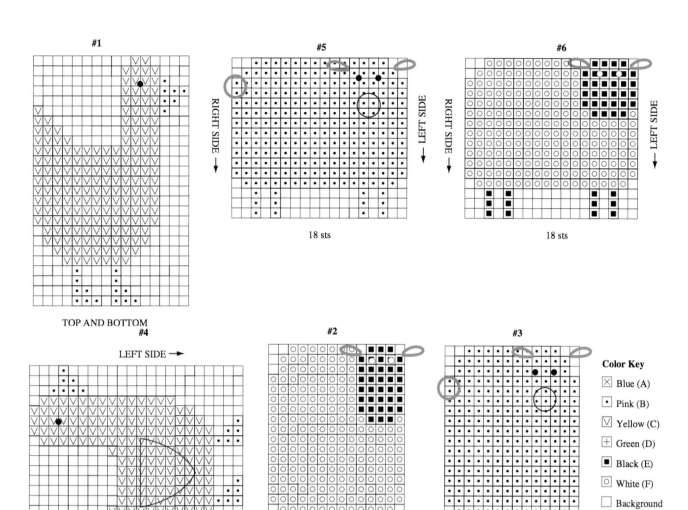

TOP AND BOTTOM

RIGHT SIDE →

LEFT SIDE →

TOP AND BOTTOM

TOP AND BOTTOM

#1 #5 #6 #4 #2 #3

18 sts 18 sts

Color Key

⊠ Blue (A)

• Pink (B)

∨ Yellow (C)

⊞ Green (D)

■ Black (E)

◎ White (F)

☐ Background

Eyes

With A, work french knot, foll chart and photo for placement.

Tail

With B, form 12-st chain lp, and tack down in a swirl. Foll chart and photo for placement.

Nose

With B, form 10-st chain loop, sew the center of loop tog and tack down. Foll chart and photo for placement.

Duck

Wing

With C, cast on 7 sts. Work in St st for 4 rows, then dec 1 st each side every other row until 1 st rem. Pull strand through lp and tack down. Foll chart and photo for placement.

Eyes

With D, work french knot, foll chart and photo for placement.

Placement Diagram

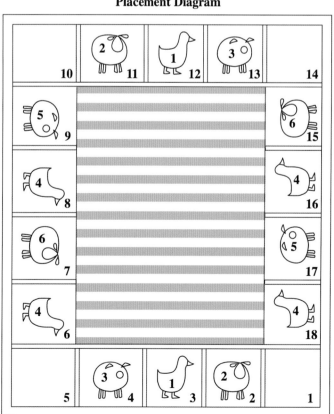

Lace Christening BLANKET

Quenet

YOU'LL NEED

YARN: ⓵ 24½oz/700g, 3080yd/ 2800m of any fingering weight cotton yarn

NEEDLES: One pair size 5 (3.75mm) needles *or size to obtain gauge*

ADDITIONAL: Cable needle (cn)

KNITTED MEASUREMENTS

• 30½"/77.5cm long x 34"/86cm wide

GAUGE

Working with 2 strands of yarn, 29-st floral pat strip is 5"/12.5cm wide, 27-st diamond pat strip is 4½"/11.5cm wide and 24-st cable pat strip is 2½"/6.5cm wide. For all strips, 34 rows to 4"/10cm.
Take time to check gauge.

Note

Blanket is worked in separate strips and sewn tog. Then edge is worked in widthwise strips and sewn on.

STITCH GLOSSARY

6-st LC Sl 3 sts to cn and hold to *front*, k3, k3 from cn.

Purl Right Dec (PRD) P1, sl 1 st knitwise, transfer back to LH needle, return purled st to LH needle and pass sl st over purled st, return to RH needle.

BLANKET

Cable Pattern Stip (make 4)

With 2 strands of yarn, cast on 24 sts. Work in cable pat foll chart, work rows 1-12 once, then cont to rep rows 3-12 (10-row rep) until strip measures 28"/71cm and there are 240 rows.
Bind off.

Floral Pattern Strip (make 2)

With 2 strands of yarn, cast on 29 sts.

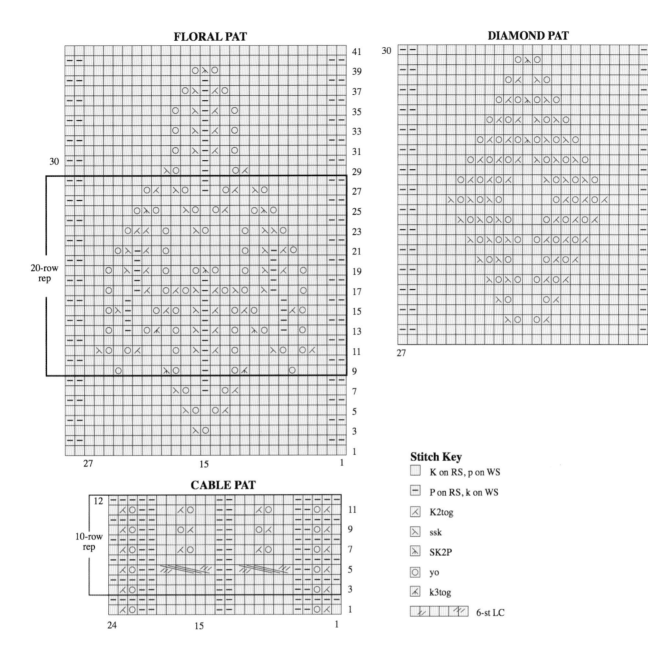

FLORAL PAT

DIAMOND PAT

CABLE PAT

Stitch Key

☐	K on RS, p on WS
−	P on RS, k on WS
⟋	K2tog
⟍	ssk
⋏	SK2P
○	yo
⋏	k3tog
⟋⟋⟋	6-st LC

Work in floral pat foll chart, working rows 1-28, then rep rows 9-27 until there are 11 reps, then work rows 29-41. Bind off.

Diamond Pattern Stip (make 1)
With 2 strands of yarn, cast on 27 sts. Work in diamond pat foll chart, rep rows 1-30 until there are 8 pat reps. Bind off.

FINISHING
Block pieces flat to measurements. Sew strips tog (see photo.)

Short-ruffled edges (make 2)
With 2 strands of yarn, cast on 172 sts.
Row 1 (RS) P1, k1, p9, *p3, k3, k2tog, [yo, k1] 8 times, ssk, k3; rep from * 6

times more, end p12, k1, p1.
Row 2 K1, p1, k9, *k3, p2, PRD, p16, p2tog, p2; rep from * 6 times more, end k12, p1, k1.
Row 3 P1, ssk (for mitered corner), p8, *p3, k1, k2tog, k16, ssk, k1; rep from * 6 times more, end p11, k2tog (for mitered corner), k1.
Row 4 K1, p1, k8, *k3, PRD, p16, p2tog; rep from * 6 times more, end k11, p1, k1. Cont to work mitered corner dec every RS row as on row 3, cont to work pat as foll:
Rows 5-16 Work rows 1-4 three times more.
Rows 17 and 18 Knit.
Rows 19 and 20 Purl.
Row 21 K3, *yo, k2tog; rep from * to last 3 sts, k3.

Rows 22 and 23 Purl.
Row 24 Knit. Bind off purlwise, dec 1 st each end.

Long-ruffled edge (make 2)
With 2 strands of yarn, cast on 193 sts. Work as for short-ruffled edges, only working rep 7 times more. When all edges are completed, block flat. Sew short edges to lower and top edges and sew long edges to side edges of blanket. Sew mitred corners tog.

Sweet DREAMS

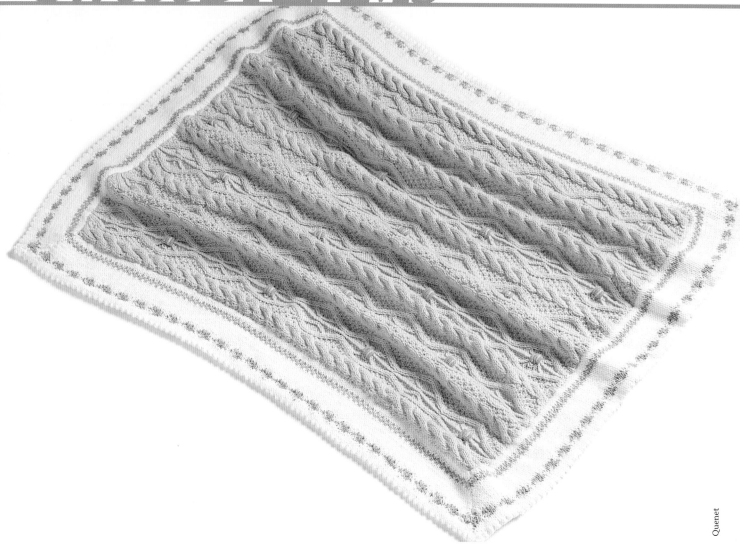

Quenet

YOU'LL NEED

YARN: 🧶3 15¾oz/450g, 1110yd/1010m of any DK weight cotton yarn in light pink (MC)

10½oz/300g, 740yd/680m of any DK weight cotton yarn in white (A)

3½oz/100g, 250yd/230m of any DK weight cotton yarn in dark pink (B)

1¾oz/50g, 130yd/120m of any DK weight cotton yarn in mint green (C)

NEEDLES: Size 6 (4mm) circular needle 36"/90cm long *or size to obtain gauge*

ADDITIONAL: Cable needle (cn)

KNITTED MEASUREMENTS
• 33" x 37"/84cm x 94cm

GAUGE
22 sts and 30 rows to 4"/10cm over St st using size 6 (4mm) needles.
Take time to check gauge.

STITCH GLOSSARY
T3B Slip next st to cn and hold to *back*, k2, then p1 from cn.
T3F Slip next 2 sts to cn and hold to *front*, p1, then k2 from cn.
Tw2L Slip next st to cn and hold to *front*, p1, then k1 tbl from cn.
Tw2R Slip next st to cn and hold to *back*, k1 tbl, then p1 from cn.

C6F Slip next 3 sts to cn and hold to *front*, k3, then k3 from cn.

BLANKET
Center Section
With MC, cast on 199 sts. Work back and forth in rows as foll:

Row 1 (RS) K1, p1, *work row 1 of cable panel over 6 sts, p1, work row 1 of diamond panel over 19 sts, p1; rep from * 6 times more, work row 1 of cable panel over 6 sts, p1, k1.

Row 2 K2, *work row 2 of cable panel, k1, work row 2 of diamond panel, k1; rep from * 6 times more, work row 2 of cable panel, k2.

Row 3 K2, *work row 3 of cable panel, k1, work row 3 of diamond panel, k1; rep from * 6 times more, work row 3 of cable panel, k2.

Row 4 K1, p1, *work row 4 of cable panel, p1, work row 4 of diamond panel, p1; rep from * 6 times more, work row 4 of cable panel, p1, K1. Cont in pats as established until 8 reps of diamond panel are complete (blanket measures approx 30"/76cm long), end with a WS row. Bind off.

FINISHING

Top or bottom edging
With RS facing and A, pick up and k 135 sts evenly across top edge of center section. P 1 row.
Next (inc) row K2, M1, k to last 2 sts, M1, k2. P 1 row.
Work border chart in St st, working inc rows as established and noting 6-st rep will be worked 22 times—159 sts. Cont with A only.
Next row (fold line - RS) K1, *yo, k2tog; rep from * to end of row. P1 row.
Next (dec) row K2, k2tog, k to last 4 sts, ssk, k2.
Rep last 2 rows 11 times more—135 sts. P 1 row. Bind off. Work in same way along bottom edge of center section.

Side edging
With RS of work facing and A, pick up and k 153 sts evenly along side edge of center section. Work as for top or bottom edging, working incs to 177 sts, then dec back to 153 sts and note 6-st rep of chart will be worked 25 times.
Bind off. Work in same way along opposite side of center section.
Sew mitered corners of edgings tog. Fold edgings in half to WS along fold line and sew in position. Embroider bullion st roses with MC and B, then embroider chain st leaves with C.
Block to measurements.

Border chart

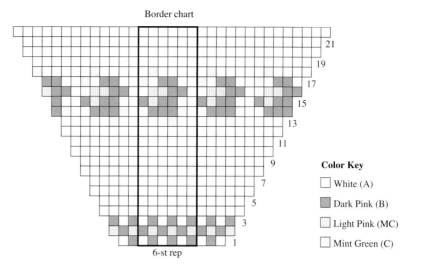

6-st rep

Color Key
- ☐ White (A)
- ▨ Dark Pink (B)
- ▨ Light Pink (MC)
- ☐ Mint Green (C)

Diamond Panel

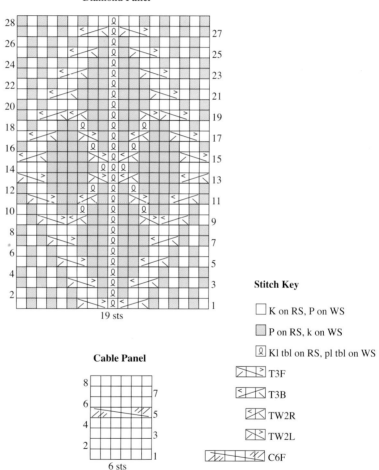

19 sts

Cable Panel

6 sts

Stitch Key
- ☐ K on RS, P on WS
- ▨ P on RS, k on WS
- Ω K1 tbl on RS, pl tbl on WS
- T3F
- T3B
- TW2R
- TW2L
- C6F

Lattice DIAMONDS

YOU'LL NEED

YARN: 🧶 12¼oz/350g, 540yd/490m of any worsted weight cotton blend yarn in grey (MC)

3½oz/100g, 160yd/140m of any worsted weight cotton blend yarn in red (CC)

NEEDLES: Size 10 (6mm) circular needle, 36"/90cm long *or size to obtain gauge*

ADDITIONAL: Cable needle (cn)

KNITTED MEASUREMENTS

• 26" x 30"/66cm x 76cm

GAUGE

18 sts and 23 rows to 5"/12.5cm over diamond cable pat using size 10 (6mm) needles.
Take time to check gauge.

STITCH GLOSSARY

4-st LC Slip next 2 sts to cn and hold to *front*, k next 2 sts, k2 from cn.

3-st LPC Slip next 2 sts to cn and hold to *front*, p next st, k2 from cn.

3-st RPC Slip next st to cn and hold to *back*, k next 2 sts, p1 from cn.

Diamond Cable Pattern (multiple of 12 sts)

Row 1 (RS) K2, p8, *4-st LC, p8; rep from * to last 2 sts, k2.
Row 2 (WS) P2, k8, *p4, k8; rep from * to last 2 sts, p2.
Row 3 K2, p8, *k4, p8; rep from * to last 2 sts, k2.
Row 4 Rep row 2.
Row 5 Rep row 1.
Row 6 Rep row 2.
Row 7 *3-st LPC, p6, 3-st RPC; rep from * to end.
Row 8 K1, p2, k6, p2, *k2, p2, k6, p2; rep from * to last st, k1.
Row 9 P1, 3-st LPC, p4, 3-st RPC, *p2, 3-st LPC, p4, 3-st RPC; rep from * to last st, p1.
Row 10 K2, p2, *k4, p2; rep from * to last 2 sts, k2.
Row 11 P2, 3-st LPC, p2, 3-st RPC, *p4, 3-st LPC, p2, 3-st RPC; rep from * to last 2 sts, p2.
Row 12 K3, p2, k2, p2, *k6, p2, k2, p2; rep from * to last 3 sts, k3.
Row 13 P3, 3-st LPC, 3-st RPC, *p6, 3-st LPC, 3-st RPC; rep from * to last 3 sts, p3.
Row 14 K4, p4, *k8, p4; rep from * to last 4 sts, k4.
Row 15 P4, 4-st LC, *p8, 4-st LC; rep from * to last 4 sts, p4.
Row 16 Rep row 14.
Row 17 P4, k4, *p8, k4; rep from * to last 4 sts, p4.
Row 18 Rep row 14.
Row 19 Rep row 15.
Row 20 Rep row 14.
Row 21 P3, 3-st RPC, 3-st LPC, *p6, 3-st RPC, 3-st LPC; rep from * to last 3 sts, p3.
Row 22 Rep row 12.
Row 23 P2, 3-st RPC, p2, 3-st LPC, *p4, 3-st RPC, p2, 3-st LPC; rep from * to last 2 sts, p2.
Row 24 Rep row 10.
Row 25 P1, 3-st RPC, p4, 3-st LPC, *p2, 3-st RPC, p4, 3-st LPC; rep from * to last st, p1.
Row 26 Rep row 8.
Row 27 *3-st RPC, p6, 3-st LPC; rep from * to end.
Row 28 Rep row 2.
Rep rows 1-28 for diamond cable pat.

BLANKET

With MC, cast on 108 sts. Work rows 1-28 of diamond cable pat 5 times, then rep rows 1 to 20 once. Piece measures approx 28"/71cm. Do not bind off. Cut MC.

Border
Note
Border is worked one edge at a time, counterclockwise around the blanket.
Row 1 With CC, k5, *k2tog, k10; rep from * to last 7 sts, k2tog, k5—99 sts.
Rows 2-6 Knit.
Bind off all sts, keeping last loop on needle (counts as first st for next border edge).
With RS facing, pick up and k 3 sts along left edge of border just worked and 120 sts down side edge of blanket—124 sts.
Row 2 Knit.
Row 3 Sl 1 st purlwise, k to end.
Row 4 Knit.
Row 5 Sl 1 st purlwise, k to end.
Row 6 Knit.
Bind off all sts, keeping last loop on needle (counts as first st for next border edge).
With RS facing, pick up and k 3 sts along left edge of border just worked and 99 sts along cast-on edge of blanket—103 sts.
Row 2 Knit.
Row 3 Sl 1 st purlwise, k to end.

Row 4 Knit.
Row 5 Sl 1 st purlwise, k to end.
Row 6 Knit.
Bind off all sts, keeping last loop on needle (counts as first st for next border edge).
With RS facing, pick up and k 3 sts along left edge of border just worked,120 sts up side of blanket and 4 sts along right edge of first border—128 sts.
Rows 2-6 Sl 1 st purlwise, k to end.
Bind off.

FINISHING
Lightly block blanket to measurements.

Quenet

Whale's TALE

Mark Zambelli

YOU'LL NEED

YARN: (**3**) 12oz/375g, 750yd/690m of any DK weight cotton in blue (A)

4oz/125g, 250yd/230m in red (B), white (C), green (D), charcoal (E), and yellow (F)

NEEDLES: Size 6 (4mm) circular needle 24" long *or size to obtain gauge*

ADDITIONAL: Size E/4 (3.5mm) crochet hook, one ⅜"/10mm white button (eye), small piece of red felt (for flag), bobbins

KNITTED MEASUREMENTS
• 28" x 40"/71cm x 101.5cm

GAUGE
20 sts and 24 rows to 4"/10cm over St st.
Take time to check gauge.

STRIPE PATTERN
*2 rows B, 2 rows C, rep from * (4 rows) for stripe pat.

Notes
1. Use a separate bobbin of yarn for each large block of color. When changing colors, twist yarns on WS to prevent holes in work.
2. Circular needles is used to accomodate large number of stitches. Blanket is worked back and forth in rows.

BLANKET
With A, cast on 141 sts. Work in garter st for 8 rows.
Next row (RS) Cont 5 sts in garter st, work in St st to last 5 sts, cont 5 sts in garter st. Cont as established, keeping 5 sts each side in garter st with A throughout, for 4½"/11.5cm above garter st, end with a WS row.

Beg charts
Next row (RS) Work 27 sts A, 20 sts chart 2, 47 sts A, 20 sts chart 1, 27 sts A. Cont as established until 19 rows of charts have been worked. Work 1 row

with A on all sts.
Next row (RS) Work 55 sts A, 31 sts chart 3, 55 sts A. Cont as established until 43 rows of chart have been worked. Work 1 row with A on all sts.
Next row (RS) Work 27 sts A, 20 sts chart 1, 47 sts A, 20 sts chart 2, 27 sts A. Cont as established until 19 rows of charts have been worked. Work with A on all sts for 4"/10cm, end with a WS row.

Beg chart 4
Next row (RS) K5 A (garter st border), work 3 sts B, [5 sts A, 3 sts B] 4 times, 2 sts A, work 50 sts chart 4, 1 st A, [3 sts B, 5 sts A] 5 times, 3 sts B, k5 A (garter st border). Cont as established, completing waves on either side of whale same as pullover (see chart 4), then cont these sts in stripe pat, until 45 rows of whale chart have been worked. Then cont all sts in stripe pat until there are 23 C stripes With A, work in garter st on all sts for 8 rows. Bind off.

FINISHING
Block piece to measurements.

Embellishments
For fish tail on green fish, with D, cast on 6 sts. Work in St st for 4 rows. Dec 1 st each side on next row, then every other row once more. Cut yarn and draw through rem 2 sts. Attach as indicated on chart 2.

For braided tail on red fish, with crochet hook, ch 1"/2.5cm and knot one end. make one each in B, D and F. Attach as indicated on chart 1.

For fish eyes, use French knots foll chart for placement and using D on chart 1 and B on chart 2.

For flag on boat, cut a piece of red felt foll chart 3 for pattern. Attach as indicated on one side.

For whale face, foll chart 5 and work chain st mouth with 3 strands B. Attach button for eye as indicated.

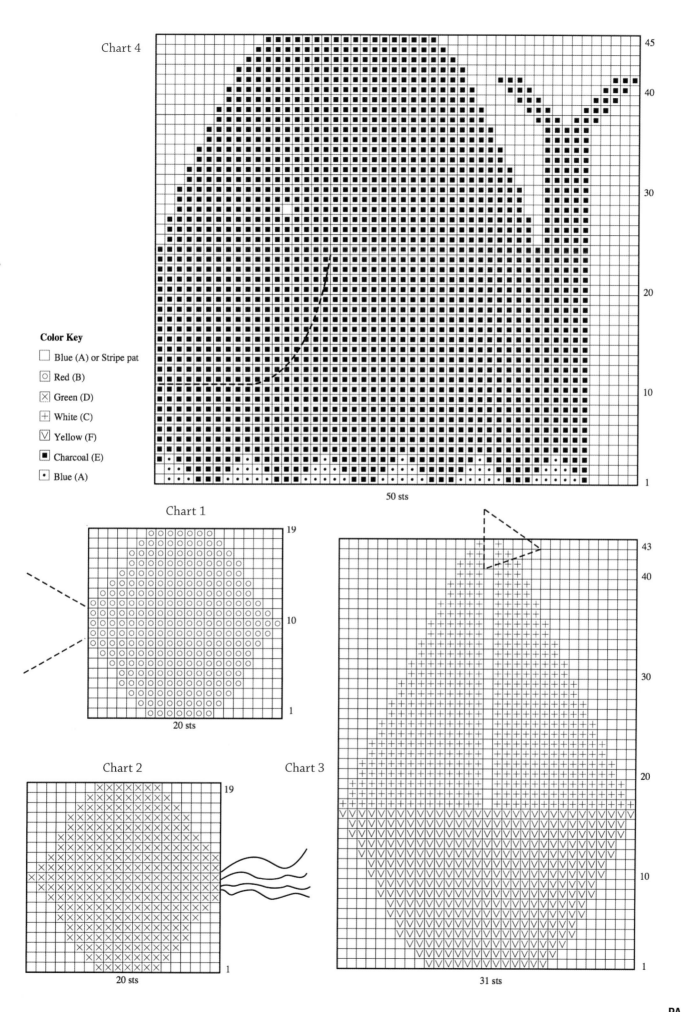

Chart 4

Color Key

☐ Blue (A) or Stripe pat

⊙ Red (B)

⊠ Green (D)

⊞ White (C)

▽ Yellow (F)

■ Charcoal (E)

⊡ Blue (A)

50 sts

Chart 1

20 sts

Chart 2

20 sts

Chart 3

31 sts

Hugs AND KISSES

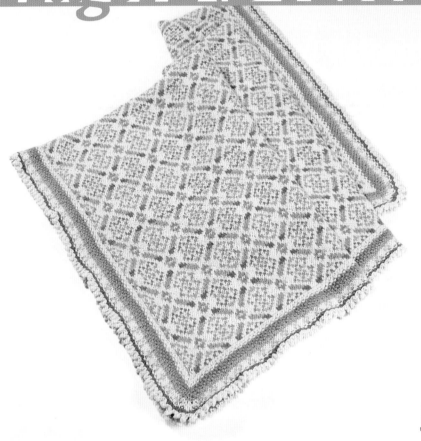

Quenet

KNITTED MEASUREMENTS
• 42"/106.5cm square

GAUGE
24 sts and 24 rows to 4"/10cm over chart pat using larger needle.
Take time to check gauge.

Note
Use two strands of E held tog throughout.

STITCH GLOSSARY
Seed Stitch in the Round (odd number of sts)
Rnd 1 *K1, p1; rep from * to last st, k1.
Rnd 2 *P1, k1; rep from * to last st, p1.
Rep rnds 1 and 2 for seed st in the rnd.
Double Inc Rnd *Work to corner st, M1, k corner st, M1; rep from * around (8 sts inc'd)

BLANKET
With larger needles and A, cast on 235 sts. Work back and forth as foll:

Beg Fair Isle chart
Row 1 (RS) Work 18-st rep of chart 13 times, work last st of chart. Cont in pat as established until 22 rows have been worked 10 times, then first 17 rows once more—piece measures approx 39½"/100cm from beg. Bind off loosley with A.

Edging
With RS facing, four smaller circular needles and A, pick up and k 1 st in each corner and 235 sts along each side edge of blanket—944 sts. Place markers before each corner st, with end of rnd marker before a corner st. Always k corner st every rnd. Join and work double inc rnd every odd rnd as foll:
Rnds 1 and 2 With A, work in seed st—952 sts. **Rnds 3 and 4** With E, work in seed st—960 sts. **Rnds 5 and 6** With D, work in seed st—968 sts.
Rnds 7 and 8 With C, work in seed st—976 sts. **Rnd 9** *M1, k corner st, M1, work 10-st rep of border chart 24 times, work first 3 sts once more; rep from * to end of rnd. **Rnds 10 and 11** Work rnds 2 and 3 of border chart, working double inc rnd on rnd 11—992 sts. **Rnd 12** With A, knit.
Rnds 13 and 14 With B, work in seed st—1000 sts. With A, work picot point bind off as foll: Bind off 2 sts, *sl rem st on RH needle to LH needle, cast on 2 sts, bind off 4 sts; rep from * to end and fasten off last st.

FINISHING
Block to measurements.

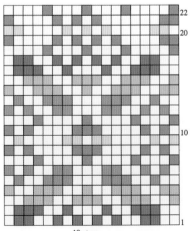

Color key
☐ Ecru (A)
▨ Teal (B)
▨ Lt blue (C)
▨ Tan (D)
▨ Rose (E)
▨ Yellow (F)

BORDER CHART

10-st rep

FAIR ISLE CHART

18-st rep